THE SEVEN
SHEPHERDS

Hanukkah in Prophecy

A BEKY Book ©

Hollisa Alewine, PhD

This booklet is a BEKY Book publication:
Books Encouraging the Kingdom of Yeshua.
www.bekybooks.com

Cover design by Rubel Photography, Mt. Juliet, TN

DEDICATION

To Charlie and Miriam, Mark and Tammy, Brother Harris and Mary, and so many others, faithful shepherds who built sukkot for the sheep.

Special Thanks to Teresa Casalino for editing assistance. We are blind to our own errors.

CONTENTS

GLOSSARY

Antiochus Epiphanes - ruler of the Seleucid Empire from 175-164 BC known for his persecution of the Jews of Judea and Samaria, which was a reversal from earlier rulers who respected Jewish culture and traditions.

Chag - a feast day or days (chagim, pl.), such as Passover, Pentecost, and Tabernacles.

Chanukkiah - an eight-branched menorah (lamp) plus one "servant" light that commemorates the victory of Chanukkah over the Greeks. In reality, the war with the Greeks continued from the time that the Temple was reclaimed from the Greeks, but the victory became the time marker for the general celebration.

Cohen HaGadol - the High Priest of Israel.

Contranym - word that functions as its own opposite, like the English word "cleave," which means both to cut away as well as to cling tightly.

Diaspora - Jews scattered into the world since the Roman exile.

Ephebion - a Greek "clubroom" or exercise room with stone benches where young men learned Greek culture.

Genesis Rabbah - a religious text from Judaism's classical period, probably written between 300 and 500 CE with some later additions. It is a midrash comprising a collection of ancient rabbinical homiletical interpretations of the Book of Genesis.

Gerousia - a council of elders.

Hellenist - a Jew influenced by Greek culture, philosophy, etc.

Judah HaMaccabee - "Judah the Hammer" was a Jewish priest and son of the High Priest Mattathias who led the Jewish revolt against the Greeks of the Seleucid Empire from 167-160 BC. He had brothers who also participated in the war against the Greeks: Jonathan, John, Simon, and Eleazer.

Kislev - the Ninth Month of the Biblical calendar; it usually falls in the Gregorian months of November or December.

Maccabee - The family of leaders of the Jewish revolt against Antiochus Epiphanes. Their army took control of Judea, and they founded the Hasmonean dynasty which ruled from 164 – 63 BC. They re-established the piety of the Jewish religion and reduced the influence of Hellenism and Hellenistic Judaism, sometimes forcing conversions to Judaism.

Maccabees I & II - two books of the Bible not typically included in modern versions, but they were included in earlier Roman Catholic Bibles. The books describe events in the "intertestamental period" between the Older and Newer Testaments.

Midrash - ancient commentary on the Hebrew scriptures. The earliest Midrashim (pl.) were written starting from the 2nd Century AD, although much of the content is older.

Moed - a feast day instructed in the Scriptures, such as Passover, Pentecost (Shavuot, Weeks), or Tabernacles (Sukkot).

Oniad - a wealthy Jewish priestly family in the early Hellenistic period. They came to prominence in Judea in the 3rd Century BC. Onias and Jason are the two most prominent members of the family who were part of a religious power struggle with the Tobiads.

Palaestra - an ancient Greek school for wrestling and boxing.

Ptolemy - the kings of the Ptolemaic Dynasty ruled the territory of Egypt after the death of Alexander the Great and division of his kingdom. Ptolemy III reigned from 246-222 BC. After a period of war in which his army reached as far as Babylon, Ptolemy III was awarded the northern coast of Syria, including Antioch.

The Red One – Esau or Edom; Rome is understood to be the descendants of Esau.

Seleucid - the kings of the Seleucid Dynasty ruled Anatolia, Persia, the Levant, Mesopotamia, and other territories in the Middle East at the height of its power. At one point, it reached as far as India. The Seleucids maintained and taught Greek culture in all their territories.

Sheni – second in number.

Shliachim – apostles, sent ones.

Sukkah - a temporary shelter or "booth" constructed to celebrate the Feast of Sukkot (Tabernacles).

Sukkot - the Feast of Tabernacles; it occurs in the fall of the year in the Seventh Month of the Hebrew calendar. It is characterized by offering first fruits of the wine vat, the threshing floor, the fruit of the ground, the fruit of the tree, and the tithes of the flocks and herds. It is celebrated by a pilgrimage to Jerusalem and living temporarily in booths for seven days.

TANAKH - Old Testament. Tanakh is an acronym for Torah, Neviim, Ketuvim, translated as Law, Prophets, and Writings, the ancient divisions of the Hebrew Bible. The books of the Tanakh are the same as, but are not arranged in the same order as Christian Bibles.

Tobiad - a priestly Jewish family faction at the beginning of the Maccabean period. The Tobiads were supporters of the Hellenistic tendencies in Judaism in the early part of the 2nd Century BC.

Ushpizin - guests. Seven messengers, or "guests" visit each family's sukkah during a daily meal at the Feast of Sukkot. They inquire as to how each person has "dwelled in sukkot." The emphasis is on caring for the poor, especially the stranger, alien, orphan, and widow.

INTRODUCTION

LEADING AND FEEDING

Before his ascension, Yeshua (Jesus) asks his disciple Peter a question three times:

> Peter, do you love me?
>
> Peter, do you love me?
>
> Peter, do you love me?

Peter responds to Messiah in the affirmative each time, and each time Yeshua commands Peter to care for his sheep. Later, as Yeshua prepares to ascend to the Father, the disciples pose a question that has kept them confused throughout Yeshua's ministry.

> So when they had come together, they were asking Him, saying, "Lord, is it *at this time You are restoring the kingdom to Israel?*" He said to them, "It is not for you to know times or epochs which the Father has fixed by His own authority; but you will receive power when the Holy Spirit has come upon you; and *you shall be My witnesses both in Jerusalem, and in all Judea and Samaria, and even to the remotest part of the earth.*"[1]

This question and Yeshua's answer is a key to unlocking the mystery of the Gentiles and Chanukkah, a victory celebration that most believe is unique to Judaism. The prophesied Messiah was to restore the kingdom

1. Acts 1:6-8

11

to Israel; that is, he was to regather the lost sheep of Israel who disappeared in various deportations by conquering empires.

Yeshua, however, had earlier hinted that there were other sheep to gather, sheep that were not of the fold of 1st Century Judaisms.[2] The Jews of the 1st Century anticipated the return of all Israel who had been lost in various deportations. They did not, however, strongly associate Messiah's gathering with those who were born strangers to the Covenant. The many bloody conquests of Israel and Judah by idolatrous Assyria, Babylon, Greece, and Rome had not left many Jews concerned with the spiritual plight of the Gentiles. Yeshua, however, refused to deal with Rome merely to prove that he was indeed the Messiah and King of the Jews. The prophetic plan was much bigger.

Messiah also must be the King of Kings of all nations, the great Shepherd to restore flocks of men [3] to the one fold of Israel as foretold in the Prophets. Had Yeshua acted at that time, the "leaven"[4] of the Holy Spirit could not work among the dough of the nations. Yeshua tells his disciples that they are a vital part of Messiah's extended work, a work intended to result in the "fullness of the Gentiles" who would hear his voice. These sheep would be found in the remotest parts of the Earth.

> This is now the third time that Jesus was manifested to the disciples, after He was raised from the dead. So when they had finished breakfast, Jesus said to Simon Peter, 'Simon, son of John, do you love Me more than these?' He said to Him, 'Yes, Lord; You know that I love You.' He said to him, 'Tend My lambs.' He said to him again a second time, 'Simon, son of John, do you love Me?' He said to Him, 'Yes, Lord; You know that I love

2. Judaism of the 1st Century was not the homogenous expression of the faith that we mostly see today. There were many sects and divisions within the sects.

3. Ez 36:38

4. Leaven is a contranym, meaning the same word has both positive and negative applications based on its context in the Word. In a negative sense, it is the hidden work of pride, envy, malice, etc. In the positive sense, it is likened to a hidden substance that permeates and grows the Kingdom of Heaven on Earth. "The kingdom of heaven is like leaven, which a woman took and hid in three pecks of flour until it was all leavened." (Mt 13:33)

You.' He said to him, 'Shepherd My sheep.' He said to him the third time, 'Simon, son of John, do you love Me?' Peter was grieved because He said to him the third time, 'Do you love Me?' And he said to Him, 'Lord, You know all things; You know that I love You.' Jesus said to him, 'Tend My sheep.'[5]

Yeshua breaks down Peter's mission into three statements known as a chiastic, or mirrored, word structure:

5. Jn 21:14-17.

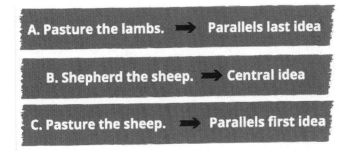

A. Pasture the lambs. ➡ Parallels last idea

B. Shepherd the sheep. ➡ Central idea

C. Pasture the sheep. ➡ Parallels first idea

When such a chiasm appears in the text, the *middle* statement (B) is the central idea. In this case (B. Shepherd the sheep), Yeshua emphasizes shepherding, which in Greek means to rule over, nourish, and feed. The first and last statements have the same verb for pasturing, specifically to feed livestock.

6. For an insightful analysis of Peter, the rock, and Yeshua, see Dr. Robin Gould's BEKY Book, *Peter's Vision: Beacon or Bacon?*

The commission of Peter[6] and the apostles is to shepherd both lambs and sheep by leading and feeding flocks of men to a Covenant relationship with God, the Stone of Israel.[7] This is to be accomplished in such a way that the sheep will be able to rest in one fold. On a simple level, lambs are those who are attached to their mothers for processed nourishment, and sheep are independent of their mothers, for they can process their food themselves. Both still need a

7. The blessing on Joseph was "... From the hands of the Mighty One of Jacob (From there is **the Shepherd, the Stone** of Israel)..." (Ge 49:24)

shepherd!

This connection with calling and nurturing both lambs and sheep is embedded in the Hebrew Prophets of the TANAKH (Older Testament). It is the identity of a shepherd that securely links the work of Messiah to the Jewish festival of Chanukkah, which in tradition carries the expectation of Micah's prophesied seven shepherds[8] who defeat the enemies of Israel.

Zechariah adds that the plan includes gathering flocks of men, not just defeating the enemy in war. This long-term prophecy explains Yeshua's resistance to calling down Heaven's army to defeat the Romans. Additionally, Zechariah's prophecy explains how Chanukkah is vital to the goal of gathering the sheep who know the Great Shepherd's voice. When the last sheep walks under Yeshua's counting staff, the Father will release Yeshua to execute judgment in the earth.

The linked prophecies of Micah, Zechariah, and Chaggai proclaim that the prophetic celebration of Chanukkah is equally as important to the lost sheep of Israel as to the native-born Jew. When Yeshua was challenged to reveal his identity during the Feast of Dedication in the Temple, his answer could not have more specifically addressed the Jewish expectation of the Seventh Shepherd to finally defeat the Red One. Both the challenge and Yeshua's answer are completely within context of the Chanukkah.

The answer, however, is not aimed only at Jews who doubted his Messiahship. It aims also at the hearts of all those who claim to hear his voice, yet they do not obey it. Those who disobey the commandments of the Great Shepherd, the Stone of Israel, are those who follow the voice of the uncircumcised heart, the "Red One." It is the rebellious sheep, both native-born and stranger, who will flee from the Great Shepherd in winter and Shabbat. Pray that *your* flight be not in winter.

8. Shabbat Minchah as extra prayer of the Modim (double Thanksgiving), p. 567 Artscroll

1

THE SHORT STORY

The Eight-day celebration of Chanukkah starting on Kislev 25 is a feast of dedication commemorating the cleansing of the Second Temple in 139 B.C. It had been made ritually unclean by idolatry and sacrifice of an unclean pig[9]; these abominations were committed by order of the Greek ruler Antiochus.

When the Holy One of Israel raised up an ordinary family to do extraordinary things, Israel was delivered from the Greeks. Judah HaMaccabee, or Judah the Hammer, and his family rose up against the oppression and idolatry of the Greek ruler. The Maccabees spearheaded the spiritual revival necessary for victory, and when the Greeks were driven off the holy mountain, the Maccabees rededicated the Temple and Israel to serve the God of Abraham, Isaac, and Jacob. Israel's God is the *Goel Yisrael*, the Redeemer of Israel. The celebration of rededication that followed is known as *Chanukkah*, or dedication. 9. See Appendix A

The ability to rededicate the Temple with holy oil in the menorah (lamp) is a cause for annual remembrance. In like manner, disciples of Yeshua stumble into unclean places in their walk and need to repent. Before the cleansing salvation of the Redeemer Yeshua, all men carried unclean thoughts and deeds in their hearts: "There is none righteous, not even one." (Ro 3:10)

THE SECOND PASSOVER

The Seed pattern [10] for Chanukkah in the Torah is the example of the Second Passover for those unable to celebrate at the appointed time, and Leviticus 23 gives two sets of instructions for the celebration of Sukkot, one for a seven-day celebration, and one with eight days.

Two kings of Israel observed double feast celebrations, a double Passover,[11] and a double Sukkot. The Prophet Haggai prophesies of an event that begins in the Ninth Month (Kislev 24), but it is based on something that happened before, when the foundations of the Temple were laid:

> Set now your heart from this day and before, from the twenty-fourth of the ninth month, back to the day when the foundations of the Sanctuary were laid; set your heart: is there any more seed in the silo? Even the grapevine and the fig tree and the pomegranate tree and the olive tree have not borne their fruit. **But from this day on I will provide blessing.**[12]

Only the celebration of Chanukkah falls on the date specified by Chaggai.

When King Solomon celebrated the inauguration of the First Temple Sanctuary, he declared a double Sukkot celebration.[13] The Prophet Haggai

10. See *Truth, Tradition, or Tare? Growing in the Word* by the author for a full discussion of the difference between growing from the Seed of the Word or adding to the Word.

11. 2 Chr 30

12. Hag 2:18

13. I Ki 8:65-66

prophesied of the 24th of Kislev as a time when a Sukkot-like blessing would begin. Haggai plants clues linking the Seed of the Torah and the celebration of Chanukkah by posing a question of the priests concerning what is "clean" or "unclean":

> Then Haggai said, 'If one who is
> unclean from a corpse touches
> any of these, will the latter become
> unclean?' And the priests answered,
> 'It will become unclean.' [14]

If a man had become unclean because of a corpse, this was the criterion for establishing a second celebration of Passover as explained in Numbers 9:9-10. Historically, Chanukkah was a late eight-day celebration of Sukkot because the Sanctuary had not been cleansed from unclean things after the war with the Greeks.[15]

This second Sukkot was known as the Feast of Dedication, and the celebration continues every year as a minor holiday. The annual commemoration is so important that in John 10:22-23, Yeshua made his declaration of unity with the Father and his dedication to call to His sheep while he was in the Temple at Chanukkah. Yeshua said His sheep would recognize his voice at Chanukkah.

Yeshua said His sheep would recognize his voice at Chanukkah.

14. Hag 2:13 (NKJV)

15. See Appendix C as well as the Books of the Maccabees

At Chanukkah, Yeshua's disciples are not walking **in** the Temple, but they **are** walking Temples of the Holy Spirit, for Yeshua called the Father's sheep out of the abominations of desolation in their lives. Sukkot is a thanksgiving celebration, and the second Sukkot, Chanukkah, also is a time for gratefulness to the One who has called mankind out of darkness into His marvelous Light. The Heavenly Father has performed great miracles in purifying the corpses of human hearts that were once dead in trespass and sin.

2

HISTORY OF CHANUKKAH

The Persian period of Israel lasted about 200 years from approximately 539 BC under Cyrus the Great to 334 or 333 BC, the time of Persia's conquest by Alexander the Great. Alexander the Great inaugurated the Hellenistic period. When he died, the generals fought for control for close to 30 years, and finally his empire was divided into three dynasties: Ptolemy, Seleucus and Antigonus.

Israel was part of the kingdom of Egypt (Macedonian Ptolemies) around 310 BC. The Ptolemies maintained at least a *de facto* control over Palestine. The country was often attacked by the Seleucids and Bedouins. Ptolemaic military units were stationed throughout Israel, and Greek cities were established. Many of these cities were set up as military colonies, and soldiers who married native women were given homes and lands. This fostered intermarriage, which was a big part of the Hellenistic culture.

Judea continued to be governed by the *Cohen HaGadol* (High Priest) and the priestly aristocracy. One of the few records from that period chronicles a dispute about taxation between High Priest Onias II and Ptolemy III Euergetes (246-221 BC).

Euergetes visited the Temple, and the result was the appointment of Joseph ben Tobiah, a nephew of the High Priest in 242 BC, as the official tax collector for the entire country. The rivalry between the Tobiad family and the Oniad family played a part in the attempt to radically Hellenize Judea later in the 2nd Century BC.

Starting in 221 BC, the Seleucid King, Antiochus III, invaded Palestine. His first attempt failed, but he persisted, and following the death of King Ptolemy IV Philopater in 203 BC, he finally succeeded in conquering in 201 BC. By 198 BC, the Seleucids were firmly in control. They would remain in power until the Maccabean Revolt (168-164 BC). By the time the Ptolemaic reign ended, Greek cities were established throughout the country, and Hellenism had a firm foundation.

When Ptolemies and Seleucids fought to gain control, Jewish factions supported each of the rivals. The *Gerousia* (council of elders) backed the Seleucids. The Cohen HaGadol, Simeon the Just, who may have headed the Gerousia, also is known to have supported the Seleucids. He was given the power over taxation which previously was assigned to Joseph ben Tobiah. Simeon the Just was charged with refurbishing the Temple and the city of Jerusalem.

Antiochus III (223-187 BC) upheld the Jewish right to live according to their ancestral laws. He confirmed the law that non-Jews could enter only the outermost area of the Temple Mount and that people afflicted with ritual impurities were excluded from the Temple precincts. However, 30 years later, his son Antiochus IV Epiphanes gained support from the Jewish proponents of extreme Hellenization, and he attempted to carry out their desire to Hellenize Jerusalem and the Jewish people.

On the eve of Hellenistic reform, the Temple was

a significant depository for funds from Jews in the Diaspora and Palestine. The Temple's position on the hill gave it great strategic value, making it a developing political and military issue as well as a religious one. Prior to Antiochus IV Epiphanes, everything connected with the Temple, including sacrifices, daily service, musical instruments, tithes, laws of ritual purity, division of the priesthood and Levites, etc., was according to the Torah.

After the conquest of Jerusalem, Antiochus IV Epiphanes was given a lavish reception by the Gerousia. He responded by exempting its members and the Temple officials from certain taxes. There is no mention of any welcome by the Cohen HaGadol. The members of the Gerousia may have included both priestly and lay leaders, the latter coming from the aristocracy closely connected with the priesthood.

This Hellenistic influence generally did not affect the Jewish peasantry. The rural inhabitants of Judea lived in small villages, farming the land and only going to the cities to sell their crops or up to Jerusalem for the festivals. It was on these occasions where they came into contact with Hellenized Jews or non-Jews. They maintained their Hebrew language and culture, yet adopted Greek words which were associated with Greek-style pottery, equipment, or tools.

The experience for Jews in the urban areas was much different. These people were mainly artisans and traders, living predominately in cities like Jerusalem. Here they had greater and much more frequent contacts with the Greek culture and their Hellenistic Jewish brethren. Living there required them to learn the Greek language to be understood.

Over time, even the traditionally observant religious Jews were affected by the Hellenistic culture. It is in this environment that certain aristocratic families connected with the priesthood pushed toward greater Hellenization. Hellenization served political and economic purposes. The Tobiad family which earlier had controlled the taxation on behalf of the Ptolemies also pushed the nation toward participating in the new world order which lay open before them.

The Jews who wanted a higher degree of Hellenization relocated to Greek cities where Greek was the everyday language and the dominant culture was Hellenistic. These Jews compromised with the pagan cults and interpreted the pagan liturgies as extensions of their own monotheistic practice. They attended the theater, sent their children to Greek schools, the gymnasium, and the *palaestra*. One room in the *palaestra* was the *ephebion* where the boys and young men sat on stone benches and learned the Greek culture. Some other rooms held boxing and wrestling instruction. Wrestling was done in the nude, and those who participated were older men, young men, and boys; therefore, homosexual encounters were prevalent. The end result was assimilation.

These Jews became known as Hellenizers, and they were willing to pay the price for economic and cultural advancement. They saw Judaism as becoming a part of the new world that Hellenistic culture was opening for them. For a time, the old order (Torah Judaism) and the new order (Hellenism) coexisted, but when the Hellenizers gained control of the Jerusalem priesthood and forced the type of Hellenism known only in the Greek cities, the stage was set for revolt.

High Priest Onias III was denounced to the Seleucid rulers. In an effort to clear his name, Onias rushed to Antioch to meet with the king. Unfortunately, King Seleucus IV died, and a more Hellenistic Antiochus Epiphanes (175-164 BC) ascended to the throne. Onias was unable to convince the new king of his loyalty, and he was forced to remain there in Antioch.

His brother Jason then purchased the priesthood from Antiochus. This disrupted the hereditary succession of the high priests.

Jason also purchased the right to establish a gymnasium and ephebion in Jerusalem, and with the cultural influence of these institutions, he thought to turn Jerusalem into a Hellenistic city-state to be called Antioch in honor of Antiochus IV. The right for the Judeans to live by Torah as previously granted by Antiochus III was rescinded. Now Jews were to live by Greek law.

The majority of those who had previously enjoyed full rights under Torah Law became second-class citizens in an oligarchy. The Greek athletic activities began, and the Gerousia was purged of members who did not support the reform. It is not surprising that the Hellenized aristocracy of Judea supported these changes. Citizenship in Greek cities held many advantages, such as the commercial benefits in trade with other cities and minting of coins.

High Priest Jason and his followers were not extremists, and they did not seek to change the Jewish faith. They maintained the Temple and its rituals according to tradition. They sought to live as Jews within the wider Hellenistic world without abandoning their ancient traditions. This was not reform enough for some. Jason was openly opposed by the Pro-Seleucid Tobiad family. He was replaced by Menelaus, who purchased the high priest's position from Antiochus in 171 BC. Jason fled Jerusalem, and once in control, Menelaus used the Temple funds to purchase gifts for Antiochus.

Menelaus's misappropriation of Temple funds and his lack of Oniad family ties caused the people to bitterly oppose him. Members of the Gerousia asked for Menelaus to be replaced, but Antiochus was not swayed. Instead he killed the representatives. Following this, popular discontent became full-scale revolt. A false rumor that Antiochus was dead brought Jason to Jerusalem to drive out Menelaus. He succeeded somewhat, but he was unable to reassert his rule. The people remembered that he was the one who started the Hellenistic reforms, and they forced him to flee Jerusalem.

Many Jews were displaced from Jerusalem when a garrison of soldiers was established. It is believed at this time that foreign deities were introduced into the Temple. The Jewish Hellenizers and Menelaus saw these gods as the equivalent to the God of Israel, and thus they believed that this was not really foreign worship. They saw the God of Israel as simply another manifestation of the supreme deity in Syria known as *Baal Shamin* (Master of Heaven) and in the Greek world as *Zeus Olympius*.

The earliest attempts at an organized uprising were led by the *Hasidim* who found the compromises totally unacceptable. In an attempt to stem the uprising, Antiochus conceived of additional persecutions. These came after years of struggle and insurrection fueled by the attempt of Hellenistic Jews to push their way of life onto the entire nation of Israel.

There is no evidence that Antiochus pursued a similar policy anywhere else in his kingdom. He saw the rebellion mounting and believed that the way to defeat it was by launching an onslaught against the very things that propelled the Jews to rebel: the Torah, the mitzvot (commandments), and the culture of the Jewish people.

About a year after Antiochus attacked Jerusalem in Kislev 167 BC, the king issued a decree that banned circumcision, Torah study, and religious observance such as Shabbat and the Biblical feasts. Antiochus desecrated the Jews' most holy site by introducing idolatrous worship in the Temple and sacrificing unclean foods on the altar (abomination of desolation).[16] As a result, Jews were forced to

16. See 2 Maccabees 6:3-6 or Appendix A

24

worship idols, eat unclean foods, and leave their sacred customs or flee into the Judean countryside.

Antiochus burned Torah scrolls and any religious writings. Women who continued to circumcise their sons were killed. The circumcised sons were hanged by the neck within their homes, and the *mohels* (men who performed circumcisions) were slain. In the ancient pagan world, this was unprecedented. Conquering kings introduced their gods to the newly conquered lands, but the people were allowed to continue in worship and customs to their gods.

Some responded by quietly acquiescing, some fled the city, but others rose up to fight. In the year following the implementation of these decrees, armed conflict broke out in Judea. It was this response that ultimately led to the reshaping of Jewish society. The uprising was led by a priest named Mattathias and his five sons, Judah Maccabee, Simon, Johanan, Eleazar, and Jonathan.

After successfully fighting Antiochus's forces, these sons reestablished Judea as a sovereign state for the first time in about 450 years, and they inaugurated a new dynasty of Jewish kings, the Hasmoneans. The name Hasmonean refers to an ancestor Mattathias, but later it became a family title for the Maccabees. These are some of the important historic developments during the intertestamental period between the writing of Malachi and Matthew.

3

TALMUDIC PAGANISM?

Like the ancient Hellenists, many generations sought to establish links among religious practices in order to assimilate into a culture that offered more tangible rewards such as economic prosperity, social acceptance, or intellectual advancement. The many parallels among religious customs encouraged assimilation, for most religious groups celebrated special holidays, fasts, or even sabbaths from ordinary work.

Because ancient cultures venerated the vital seasonal changes associated with crops, most have both "spring" and "fall" celebrations as well as acknowledgments of the winter solstice. Pagan myths offer parallel narratives or symbols, such as the myth of Achilles' heel, which has a thematic connection to the Biblical prophecy (Ge 3:15) concerning the offspring of Eve, offspring vulnerable at the heel.

Because there are so many parallels and overlapping themes, to those who seek to justify fusing their own beliefs or practices to new ones, it is not difficult to find the similarities. On the other hand, it is impossible to ignore the distinct differences. Rabbi

David Fohrman's lectures [17] on Chanukkah point out some curious similarities between pagan ritual and Jewish traditions in the winter holidays. The text of these discussions is found in the *Talmud*,[18] a comprehensive historical documentation of Jewish law and practice.

The discussions are found in two tractates, Shabbos and Avodah Zara. A brief summary of points follows:

SHABBOS 22a	AVODAH ZARA 8a
The rabbis ask, "What is Chanukkah?" They caution Jews not to deliver eulogies or fast. Then comes the story of Chanukkah.	Discusses two pagan holidays, warning Israelites to avoid them: Kalanda and Saturnura. Adam fasted and prayed for eight days because he thought the shortening winter days was the onset of his promised death.
The year after the lighting of the menorah with the last sealed vessel of oil, the holiday of Chanukkah was established. The *chanukkiah* is lit with increasing light over eight days.	Darkness had increased during Adam's eight-day mourning time, but then light increased after the solstice.
Worship and thank the God of Israel.	Adam established eight more days, but for the celebration of deliverance the next year. The pagans who came after, however, appropriated the mourning and thanksgiving celebration to worship the stars.

17. Aleph Beta Institute

18. See S. Creeger's BEKY Book *Introduction to the Jewish Sources* for a brief history and summary of the ancient Jewish sources.

There are some similarities between the Jews' record of events to the pagan winter solstice practices, but the point is to establish the differences by acknowledging the similarities. In cases where there is a temptation to merge a Bible-based practice with a practice from the nations, the similarity must be acknowledged so that the difference is exposed.

Fasting and praying are two similar actions, but the sages caution the Jews against fasting or excessive mourning at this season. Both holidays occur at a time of diminishing daylight. The Jewish holiday, though, occurs at a time fixed according to the lunar reckoning of Biblical months, and the pagan holiday occurs according to the solar-influenced calendar.

Rabbi Fohrman points out the differences hinted to in the *Talmud*: while Adam's first winter experience deduced the lengthening of the daylight to be a normal cycle of nature, the Jews attributed the lengthening of the lamplight to God's miraculous intervention in the realm of nature. Fasting and mourning during the short days of winter is a custom common among ancient pagan religious practices.

To the Jewish mind, it is not the stars or foreign gods who control the annual seasons, but the Creator of the Universe, the Elohim (God) of Abraham, Isaac, and Jacob. Elohim doesn't merely set the universe in motion and remove Himself from its daily operation; instead, He can be invited by mankind to intervene in a supernatural way in times of distress and spiritual renewal.

How old is this Biblical pattern of supernatural intervention in the lives of ordinary people? Although there are other events recorded in Scripture, one event is significant in relation to Chanukkah. It is a thanksgiving celebration of miraculous light for salvation: the burning bush.

4

HOW ALEXANDER'S HORRIBLE, NO GOOD, VERY BAD DAY BECAME A CHANUKKAH CELEBRATION

One key event in Israelite history that involved a miraculous, great light was the burning bush:

> Now Moses was pasturing the flock of Jethro his father-in-law, the priest of Midian; and he led the flock to the west side of the wilderness and came to Horeb, the mountain of God. The angel of the LORD appeared to him in a blazing fire from the midst of a bush; and he looked, and behold, **the bush was burning with fire**, **yet the bush was not consumed.** So Moses said, 'I must turn aside now and see this marvelous sight, why the bush is not burned up.' When the LORD saw that he turned aside to look, God called to him from the midst of the bush and said, 'Moses, Moses!' And he said, 'Here I am.' [19]

19. Ex 3:1-4

An Israelite fugitive from Egypt is pasturing his father-in-law's sheep in the wilderness at the "mountain of God." The angel appears to this ordinary shepherd, but the LORD does not speak to the shepherd Moses until he turns aside to consider the miraculous fire burning. It is at this point that an ordinary shepherd is called to do something extraordinary: deliver the Israelites from the control of Egypt.

Presented with a supernatural light, Moses becomes a great light of salvation to his people. He becomes a greater shepherd, a shepherd of flocks of people. Moses was able to lead out of tribulation both Israel and the mixed multitude of sheep, for a mixed multitude of Gentiles left Egypt with Moses. Two flocks, one shepherd. Moses encounters the miraculous fire on the Mountain of God on two journeys: with the sheep of his father-in-law and with the sheep of his Father in Heaven, or Father-in-[Torah] Law.

Moses asks why (*maduah?*) the bush is not burning. The Hebrew word *maduah* does not just mean why, but what is the *process*? What happened *in the past* to make this happen? In order to realize a bush is not being consumed, one would have to spend some time, wait, and consider the process. Moses infers that the fire is not an earthly fire. It came about through a different *process*. The bush was not the fuel for the fire, just like the oil was not the fuel for the menorah.

In the same manner, victory and miracles can be seen by turning aside to alleviate human suffering and acknowledging the intervention of Adonai in this physical world. This is drawing near the Mountain of God. This is the fiery Torah (law) that comes down from Heaven, not from the physical world. Supernatural fire comes down to cause mankind to turn aside, consider, and draw near to Adonai as well as to care for the sheep of the Father.

20. For a full explanation of Moses' excuse that he has uncircumcised lips, see BEKY Book *The Circumcision Circumvention Circumvision.*

The supernaturally-burning bush becomes the

symbol of inspiration to a very reluctant Moses,[20] who doubts his ability to become a messenger of salvation. Moses probably never thought he'd become the instrument through which the God of Abraham, Isaac, and Jacob would once again save His people from idolatry. It was a difficult job, for with the Golden Calf, the Israelites demonstrated the depths of assimilation to which they had sunk under Egypt's influence. They were a nation in need of rededication to the Elohim whom their fathers had served.

It also is likely that Moses, a descendant of Levi, never envisioned establishing a priesthood through his brother Aaron in Israel, but in his zealous actions to rid the nation of syncretized worship, Moses calls the Levites to take up a sword. The Levites stood against their unrepentant brothers calling the golden calf the God who brought them out of Egypt. They were not the same God! Similarities do not equal the same identity, just as the Talmud instructs Jews concerning the differences between Chanukkah and pagan rituals.

Many hundreds of years later, Mathias Maccabee's Jewish priestly family rose up from their place of exile in northwest Judea to wage a guerilla war against the Greeks and Hellenist Jews, and they regained control of the Temple, removing the foreign gods. The Israelites under the Maccabees' leadership attack both Greeks and Hellenist Jews, and Judah Maccabee's brother takes the office of High Priest to cleanse the Temple. It is from this historic event that the modern legend of the miraculously burning fire is drawn, but its roots in the burning bush are much older.

In fact, many people who celebrate Chanukkah today are not even aware of a Chanukkah miracle that occurred 150 years earlier than the Maccabees'. In that miracle, the metaphor of "great lights" as leaders inspiring an assembly of people[21] shines as

21. Each of the seven assemblies addressed in the Book of Revelation is to be inspired by a "messenger" or "angel." These messengers are to inspire each of the seven to specific works of patience or repentance. Since the seven assemblies also are represented by the seven-branched menorah before the Throne, they also are called to be "great lights." The symbolic relationship given as an example to Thyatira was "that Jezebel woman" who enticed the Israelites to eat things sacrificed to idols, also the sin of the Nicolaitans. In other words, they syncretized the worship of the Holy One of Israel with foreign practices.

33

a better conclusion to Greek encroachment upon the descendants of Jacob.

This earlier Chanukkah miracle is recorded in Yoma 69a of the Talmud. The legal discussion centers upon the question of whether the Cohen HaGadol (High Priest) is allowed to wear the priestly garments outside the Temple. Although the context seems an unlikely place to find information about the miraculous lights of Chanukkah 150 years later in the Temple, the contextual clues link the priesthood, long-burning fire, and the relationship of the native-born Israelite to the nations. The context also alludes to an apostate, ethno-religious subset of Israelites, the Samaritans.

The Samaritans have much in common with the Jews, including the Torah as their foundational religious document. The Samaritans were the offspring of Israelites who married other peoples. These other peoples were sent by Assyrian conquerors to populate Israel and to ensure it stayed under the control of the conquering empire. The Samaritans, however, had their own priesthood and worshiped on Mount Gerizim, not the Temple Mount in Jerusalem. They were antagonistic to the Jews and vice versa.

One bit of mischief that the Samaritans perpetrated was setting false signal fires around the first of each month so that Jews would be confused as to the first day of the lunar month. Once the new moon was sighted and certified in Jerusalem, signal fires relayed around the country to notify everyone to synchronize their calendars with the new month. By setting false signal fires, the Samaritans disrupted the synchronization of both the practical calendar as well as the worship calendar that kept Jews celebrating in unity.

Alexander the Great was persuaded by the Samaritans (Cutheans) to destroy the Jewish Temple, and he and his army marched on Jerusalem to subdue the rumored rebellion. Hearing of this horrible plan, the Cohen HaGadol, Shimon HaTzaddik, took counsel with the prominent Jewish leaders. With great courage, Shimon HaTzaddik put on the High Priest's garments, and he and the elders went out to meet Alexander. They marched all night with torches to intercept Alexander's army. According to tradition, the torches miraculously did not go out during the long night march.[22]

When Alexander the Great saw the Cohen HaGadol at daybreak, he bowed before him, causing great distress to his officers and men. They asked why he would bow before a Jew, and Alexander replied that he had seen Simon HaTzaddik in a vision before he would go into battles. He saw the High Priest as a sign of success from God, so he spared the Jews and Temple, and he gave the Samaritans over to the very destruction that they had planned for the Jews. The reversal is very much like the one recorded in the Book of Esther where those who intended the Jews harm were instead put to the sword. Just as Queen Esther answers the king's question as to whom would want to do her people harm, so the High Priest identifies the mischief makers, the Cutheans.

One quotation from Yoma 69a is tied to the reasoning that Jews should not fast and mourn at the time of the winter solstice. When the High Priest Simon HaTzaddik confronts Alexander, he asks:

> Is it possible that *star-worshippers* should mislead you to destroy the House wherein prayers are said for you and your kingdom that it be never destroyed! He said to them: Who are these? They said to him: These are Cutheans who stand before you. He [Alexander] said: They are delivered into your hand.

Simon HaTzaddik calls the Samaritans (Cutheans)

22. For another supernatural account of fire, see Appendix B

"star worshippers." To the rabbis of the Talmud, there was a difference between the Jewish celebration of Chanukkah as one of supernatural intervention in the course of nature and the pagan celebrations defined by Adam's descendants. The pagan celebrants turned the natural event into star worship with times of mourning.[23] Like the Israelites who syncretized the golden calf of Egypt with YHVH (God) and the Jewish Hellenists who syncretized pagan worship with Temple worship, the High Priest points out which side of celebration the hybrid Israelite Samaritans had chosen, calling them star-worshippers.

Figure 1
Drawing of an ancient synagogue mosaic.

23, See chart in chapter on "Talmudic Paganism?"

24. Original photograph may be viewed at http://www. national geographic. com.au/history/ does-this-mysterious-mosaic-portray-alexander-the-great.aspx

Figure 1 is a drawing made from a photograph recently excavated from a synagogue in Huqoq, Israel.[24] The mosaic depicts a Greek military king (possibly Alexander) speaking with a Jewish noble or priest. The Greek commander's army is accompanied by elephants, a Greek military trademark. The Jewish nobles hold swords, possibly to execute judgment on the Cutheans. Of note is the lower part of the mosaic. It is an arrangement of the eight nobles standing equidistant from the nobleman seated in the middle of them, creating a kind of human menorah, or chanukkiah.

Although Jewish thought sounds ethnocentric in regard to non-Jews and Israelites who assimilate into neighboring cultures, their ability to incorporate the mixed multitude from Egypt or the righteous converts like Rahab and Ruth speaks to a covenant of inclusion. As long as the stranger is willing to come close to the covenant of the Torah instead of replace or fuse it to pagan customs, there is a path of inclusion.

> **As long as the stranger is willing to come close to the covenant of the Torah instead of replace or fuse it to pagan customs, there is a path of inclusion.**

Significantly, the Talmud records: "Surely it was taught: The twenty-fifth of Tevet is the day of Mount Gerizim, on which no mourning is permitted." The date and non-mourning clause in the tenth month are significant, for the "second" Chanukkah of the Maccabees was commemorated exactly one month earlier, on the 25th of Kislev, the ninth month. Although the dates are separated by one month and 150 years, the link between celebrations on the 25th of the ninth and tenth months is called a *sheni* in Hebrew. The sheni (second) becomes a significant clue based in the Torah and expanded in later books.

At the first Chanukkah, Alexander reversed his decision, grateful to meet the Cohen HaGadol of his dreams, and the first meeting of Greek and Jewish culture was a positive one. The horrible, no good, very bad day planned for the Jews became a celebration. It was generations later that the Greeks once again persecuted the Jews who kept the Torah and worshipped in Jerusalem.

What is the significance of the "first" Chanukkah celebrated when Alexander the Great turned from a decree of destruction against the Jewish Temple? In the Talmud, this story is told in relation to a halakhic question, "Can the Cohen HaGadol wear the priestly garments outside the Temple?" The sages answer, "Yes, he can." Garments of salvation can be revealed to the nations and result in peace, hence, the House of God will be a House of prayer for all nations.

In the rabbinic literature of the Gemara and Midrash, for the 40 years that Shimon HaTzaddik was Cohen HaGadol, the westernmost branch of the menorah miraculously always burned even though the other lamps burned through their supplies of oil. The Western lamp was "*maarav*," which means its wick pointed to the West. The root of *maarav* means "mixture." The righteous among the nations would be welcomed into the native-born People of the Book. The tribe of Ephraim became a symbol of this mixture, for his tribal camp was on the Western side of the Tabernacle, and after his dispersion, "Ephraim mixes himself with the nations..."[25]

The potentially horrible, no good, very bad day for both Alexander and the Jews was averted when a wise High Priest put on his holy garments and revealed himself to a prince among nations, bringing salvation to both Jews and Greeks. The meeting of the miraculous light occurred 150 years *and one month* before the Chanukkah Sheni that is celebrated today. The Chanukkah commemorated today

25. Ho 7:8

38

also is a day of Thanksgiving, but the thanksgiving is offered after a *war* with the Greeks, not peace. The Thanksgiving of the first Chanukkah is that there was no war because of the High Priest who revealed his garments to the Gentiles.

> Seeing then that we have a great
> high priest, that is passed into the
> heavens, Jesus the Son of God, let us
> hold fast our profession.[26]

The noblemen and Cohen HaGadol who marched with their torches all night at the risk of their lives were great lights; those great lights were messengers of peace to the nations.

Possible Chiastic (mirror) Structure

Pesach	Pesach Sheni		Chanuk-kah Sheni?	Chanuk-kah
		Av 5th Month		

| 14/15 Nisan 1st Month | 14/15 Ziv 2nd Month | | 25 Kislev 9th Month | 25 Tevet 10th Month |

Figure 2
A sample chiastic structure

Figure 2 suggests a chiastic structure. The seed of the sheni is found in the instructions concerning a second Passover in the 1st and 2nd months, so it is used as one boundary of the chiasm. The celebration in question, Chanukkah, and its "sheni" occur in the 9th and 10th months. This highlights the axis of the chiasm, the month of Av, the 5th month.

26. He 4:14

Av is considered the most tragic month on the Hebrew calendar. The High Priest Aaron died on the first of Av (Nu 33:38). Both the First and Second Temples were destroyed on the 9th of Av. The Israelites cried on the 9th of Av when the evil spies brought back a faithless report. Believing that it was impossible to live in the Land of Israel, they wanted to go back to Egypt. In more modern history, the Jews were expelled from England and Spain on the 9th of Av. The false messiah, Simon bar Kokhba, was defeated by Rome on the 9th of Av, and Jews were cruelly slaughtered.

In synagogues there are weekly readings from the Torah and the Prophets. The reading from the Prophets is called a *haftarah*. In the Three Weeks of Sorrow leading up to the 9th of Av, the *haftorot* (pl.) are readings of punishment, but from the 9th of Av until the Feast of Trumpets, there are seven weeks of reading haftorot of comfort. The Torah portions Mattot and Masei, which describe the apportioning of the Land of Israel, are read during the Weeks of Sorrow in order to encourage Israel during its time of reflection on past destructions. Although Israel may be in exile, the Messiah will return them to their tribal inheritances.

The month of Av is often called *Menachem Av*, which means "Comfort of the Father," for the readings remind Israel of the ultimate regathering of her exiles. The Prophet Jeremiah instructs Israel to assign land to the stranger who chooses to dwell in the Land; the stranger can choose the tribe with whom he chooses to live:

> 'So you shall divide this land among
> yourselves according to the tribes
> of Israel. You shall divide it by lot for
> an inheritance among yourselves
> and among the aliens who stay
> in your midst, who bring forth sons
> in your midst. And they shall be to
> you as the native-born among the

sons of Israel; they shall be allotted
an inheritance with you among
the tribes of Israel. And in the tribe
(*shevet*) with which the alien (*ger*)
stays, there you shall give him his
inheritance,' declares the Lord GOD.
[27]

The *ger* (stranger) may elect to join himself to the
shivtei (tribes) of Israel. The month of the "first"
Chanukkah, the 10th of Tevet, precedes the month
of Shevat. In the month of Tevet, Queen Esther was
taken into King Ahaseurus's palace, and one year
later in the month of Tevet, she was chosen to be
Queen over 127 provinces. The matriarch Sarah, who
was 127 years old when she died, was prophesied to
be a mother of many nations. In the month of Tevet,
Queen Esther became the Queen Mother of those
prophetic nations.

It was under Queen Esther's rule that the Jews among
those nations were saved from the enemy, yet many
non-Jews began to identify themselves as Jews:

> In each and every province and
> in each and every city, wherever
> the king's commandment and his
> decree arrived, there was gladness
> and joy for the Jews, a feast and
> a holiday. *And many among the
> peoples of the land became Jews*,
> for the dread of the Jews had fallen
> on them.[28]

On Tevet 24 in the 3rd Century BC, the Hebrew Bible
was translated into Greek and became available to
many nations. In generation after generation, the
Scriptures offer a pattern of inclusion to the nations.
Although Jews continue to celebrate Purim and
Chanukkah, the celebrations have as much to do
with the salvation of the non-Jew as the Jew:

27. Ez 47:21-23

28. Es 8:17

41

The Jews established and made a
custom for themselves and for their
descendants *and for all those who
allied themselves with them*, so that
they would not fail to celebrate
these two days according to their
regulation and according to their
appointed time annually.

*So these days were to be
remembered and celebrated
throughout every generation*, every
family, every province and every
city; and these days of Purim were
not to fail from among the Jews,
or their memory fade from their
descendants. (Es 9:27-28)

By continuing to celebrate Purim in every generation,
Jews, and "all who allied themselves with them" shine
a light of salvation to the Gentiles. Esther is a book
in which God's name is not mentioned even once.
He is hidden, but present and working, like the good
leaven of the Holy Spirit. Miracles, like prophecies,
are sometimes hidden from plain view at the time
they occur, but they are evident later.

Although most sources read that the name of the 11th
month, Shevat, which follows Tevet, came from the
Akkadian language, it is spelled exactly the same as
the Hebrew word for tribe, *shevet*. What follows the
deliverance of Israel in Tevet? The assignment of the
native Israelite tribes to their ancestral Land, Israel.
In Messianic times, however, the strangers who have
joined themselves to Israel will join those tribes and
become one with the tribe and nation.

Within the traditions of the chiastic axis, the month
of Av, is a key theme. The nickname *Menachem Av*
encourages Israel in every place of exile. What is
the Comfort of the Father? Yeshua points out to his
disciples that in their mission to take the message of

the Jewish Messiah into the world of the stranger, the comforting Father will send something needful. That something is The Comforter, the Holy Spirit:

> But *the Comforter, which is the Holy Ghost, whom the Father will send in my name,* he shall teach you all things, and bring all things to your remembrance, whatsoever I have said unto you.[29]

29. Jn 14:26

5

GREAT LIGHTS

Lights ≈ People

Lights ≈ Assemblies of People

The chanukkiah represents miracles, deliverance, and even the Holy Spirit, for any intervention from The Holy One is the work of the Holy Spirit. God is not a man, but a Spirit, and the seven-branched menorah is identified in the Book of Revelation as a representation of both the Seven Spirits of Adonai as listed in Isaiah *as well as* a representation of seven assemblies of people.

This is another key to understanding the eight[30] lights of Chanukkah. An eight-branched menorah (*chanukkiah*) is a metaphor for eight people, or in the metaphoric language of Yeshua and the apostles, "lights in the world."

> Do all things without grumbling or disputing; so that you will prove yourselves to be blameless and innocent, children of God above

30. There are actually nine branches including the "servant" branch, which lights the other eight.

reproach in the midst of a crooked and perverse generation, among whom *you appear as lights in the world*, holding fast the word of life. [31]

Early Church records refer to the early apostles as "great lights," and Eusebius cites Polycrates, who spoke of seven specific great lights:

For in Asia also *great lights* have fallen asleep, which shall rise again on the day of the Lord's coming, when he shall come with glory from heaven, and shall seek out all the saints. Among these are *Philip*, one of the twelve apostles, who fell asleep in Hierapolis; and his *two aged virgin daughters, and another daughter*, who lived in the Holy Spirit and now rests at Ephesus; and, moreover, *John*, who was both a witness and a teacher, who reclined upon the bosom of the Lord, and, being a priest, wore the sacerdotal plate. He fell asleep at Ephesus. And *Polycarp* in Smyrna, who was a bishop and martyr; and *Thraseas*, bishop and martyr from Eumeneia, who fell asleep in Smyrna...(Eusebius, Church History, Book V, Chapter 24)

The lights of the menorah more literally represent the Seven Spirits of Adonai as listed in Isaiah and Revelation:

Then a shoot will spring from the stem of Jesse, and a branch from his roots will bear fruit. The Spirit of the LORD will rest on Him, the spirit of wisdom and understanding, the spirit of counsel and strength, the spirit

31. Phillipians 2:14-16

46

of knowledge and the fear of the
LORD.[32]

Out from the throne come flashes
of lightning and sounds and peals
of thunder. And there were seven
lamps of fire burning before the
throne, which are the seven Spirits of
God...[33]

The golden seven-branched menorah of Israel's
Tabernacle had several important features. First,
it was one piece of beaten gold symbolizing
indivisibility, eternity, permanence, and superiority to
all other substances (Ryken, Wilhoit, & Longman, p.
341). This reminded the priests who tended it morning
and evening that it was man's responsibility to be a
faithful vessel of the Seven Spirits of Elohim on Earth
at all times.

The lamp was to be kept burning continually to
combat the forces of spiritual darkness and chaos
that strive against the Spirit of God. Did the lamp
represent the Spirit of Adonai to Israel, or did the lamp
represent the Spiritual service of Israel to Adonai and
to the nations? Yes. Both!

The indivisibility of the lamp was a symbol of the
unity of the comforting Holy Spirit. The Seven Spirits
of Adonai were not separate from His One Holy
Spirit. Another paradox is seen within the menorah's
structure. It represents light, which is uncontained,
yet the light is contained in the vessel of the lamp.
"The commandment is a lamp and the Torah is
a light"[34] illustrates this twofold expression. Most
importantly, the seven-branched menorah in the
Tabernacle represented the infinite light of Adonai
illuminating a finite world.

The blossoming branches of the menorah
demonstrate the ability of the Holy Spirit to bear
fruit in the Creation, the fruit of the Spirit. Because

32. Is 11:1-2

33. Re 4:5

34. Pr 6:23

47

Adam was made in the image of his spiritual Creator, Adonai and man share a lamp that operates inside of the man:

> The spirit of a man is the lamp of the
> LORD, searching all the inner depths
> of his heart.[35]

These human bodies of flesh can be very good vessels for the Seven Spirits of God when human beings make choices consistent with His teachings; doing so shines His Holy Spirit in the Earth to preserve it. It is not a bad thing to be "in the flesh" because it means we are still alive, but it is a bad thing to be in the flesh when its appetites overrule the creative Spirit of Elohim.[36]

Yeshua was present at the Creation and was the source of any Creation that occurred. Yeshua was the Beginning of "in the beginning":

> To the angel of the church in
> Laodicea write: the Amen, the
> faithful and true Witness, the
> Beginning of the creation of God,
> says this...[37]

> In the beginning was the Word,
> and the Word was with God, and
> the Word was God. He was in the
> beginning with God. All things came
> into being through Him, and apart
> from Him nothing came into being
> that has come into being.[38]

> He is the image of the invisible God,
> the firstborn of all creation.[39]

35. Pr 20:27

36. Elohim is the name of God the Creator used in the Hebrew Bible

37. Re 3:14

38. Jo 1:1-3

39. Col 1:15

40. Ps 97:11

The seeds of light were sown for the righteous by the Creator on Day One.[40] Those seeds, however, contained the potential for all types of "bodies," or vessels for that seed of light. Paul discusses this in his letter to the Corinthians. Each vessel of Creation would bear a particular kind of glory or radiance that illuminated the handiwork of its Creator.

> And that which you sow, you do not sow the body which is to be, but a bare grain, perhaps of wheat or of something else. But God gives it a body just as He wished, and to each of the seeds a body of its own. All flesh is not the same flesh, but there is one flesh of men, and another flesh of beasts, and another flesh of birds, and another of fish. There are also heavenly bodies and earthly bodies, but the glory of the heavenly is one, and the glory of the earthly is another. There is one glory of the sun, and another glory of the moon, and another glory of the stars; for star differs from star in glory.[41]

A human being's job is to act in harmony with his type of vessel so that it may radiate the glory-light of Elohim! A human being's eyes can reflect the extent to which the lamp of God has been allowed to give light and to increase spiritual vision. If the Torah is a light and the commandment a lamp, then the eye of the human body represents the spiritual commandments.

> The eye is the lamp of your body; when your eye is clear, your whole body also is full of light; but when it is bad, your body also is full of darkness. Then watch out that the light in you is not darkness. If therefore your whole body is full of light, with no dark part in it, it will be wholly illumined, as when the lamp illumines you with its rays.[42]

41. I Co 15:37-40

42. Lu 11:34-36

49

In Yeshua's exhortation to his disciples, he cautions them that their lights could be darkness. This would diminish their ability to be a light to the nations:

> I am the LORD, I have called you in
> righteousness, I will also hold you by
> the hand and watch over you, and
> I will appoint you as a covenant to
> the people, as a light to the nations.
> [43]

> Nations will come to your light, and
> kings to the brightness of your rising.
> [44]

Being a light in Scripture requires righteousness, obedience, and humility like Yeshua's, but this is how the nations are drawn to the light of the Kingdom. A lampstand of seven branches represents both the Seven Spirits of Adonai and His people:

> As for the mystery of the seven stars
> which you saw in My right hand,
> and the seven golden lampstands:
> the seven stars are the angels of
> the seven churches, and **the seven
> lampstands are the seven churches**.
> [45]

43. Is 42:6

44. Is 60:3

45. Re 1:10-11

46. In the diaspora (outside the Land of Israel) a ninth day of Sukkot is celebrated; it is called *Simchat Torah*, or Rejoicing in the Torah.

If the menorah of Israel had seven branches, then why would a nine-branched (the ninth is the *shamash*: "servant branch" [46]) menorah, called a *chanukkiah*, be used for the celebration of Chanukkah? The obvious answer is that it commemorates eight days of dedication, but the clue of consecutive numbers in Scripture provides a link to a deeper level of understanding.

There is a subtle textual technique used in Scripture that presents consecutive numbers that signal a transition from the more literal and physical level to a spiritual explanation of the concept. For instance,

> Divide your portion to seven, or even
> to eight, for you do not know what
> misfortune may occur on the earth.
> [47]

This is good advice, yes, but here the writer hints to an earthly misfortune that requires a division of eight, rather than seven, portions. While the number seven represents the completion of the created world, the number eight signifies a new beginning without the veil of flesh. This is symbolized by circumcision which takes place on the eighth day of life. The Book of Revelation prophesies a release of Satan at the conclusion of the seventh millennium, which is a misfortune on the earth, so Heavenly wisdom dictates that the righteous be apportioned an eighth day.

An additional consecutively-numbered theme is in Micah 5:5, which hints to Chanukkah. It is easy to see the metaphor of eight lights representing eight people:

> This One will be our peace.
> When the Assyrian invades our land,
> When he tramples on our citadels,
> Then we will raise against him
> *Seven shepherds and eight leaders*
> *of men.*

Consecutive numbering is one method of interpreting Scriptural metaphors, but locating the seed thoughts in the Torah establishes roots to the origin of Chanukkah's eight-light Temple dedication.

How about the birth order of King David as another example? The text of 1 Samuel 16:10-11 implies that Jesse, the father of Israel's King David, had eight sons, of which David was the eighth. But 1 Chronicles 2:13-15 only names seven sons, and David was the youngest. How many sons did Jesse really have? The easy answer is that one of the sons may have died, and he was not named in the genealogies. In

47. Ec 11:1

that respect, David would have been BOTH seventh and eighth in birth order. In the realm of the earthly misfortune, he would have been the surviving seventh son; in the realm of the spirit, the missing brother still exists, and David was the eighth.

The eight-branched menorah with its *shamash* (servant) candle never represented a replacement for the seven-branched menorah of the Tabernacle. Many Orthodox Jews do not have a seven-branched candelabra in their homes precisely because they want to avoid replicating the Tabernacle's lamp. This is derived from Exodus 30, which prohibits trying to copy the anointing oil and incense used in the Tabernacle for personal use. By extension, some Jews use a chanukkiah for decoration instead of a menorah in order not to inadvertently violate the instructions of Exodus 30. Far from "adding to" the commandments of God, Jews are being careful to avoid breaking one.

SHENI

The last commanded feast of the Biblical year is Sukkot (The Feast of Tabernacles), and its celebration requires one week plus an eighth day called *Shemini Atzeret*. Even the first feast, Passover, has a "hidden" eighth day not mentioned directly in the Leviticus text. The collection of the *chametz*,[48] which is a ritual of Passover, is on the eve of the 14th of Nisan; Nisan is the first Hebrew month, and it falls in the spring.

In the Book of Chaggai (Haggai), the prophecy of Chanukkah is juxtaposed with symbols of the seven-day *chag* (feast) of Sukkot.[49] Or is it eight days? Leviticus 23 intentionally gives two sets of directions to Sukkot, one for seven days, and one for eight.

The eighth day is described in more detail first in Leviticus 23: 34-36:

> Speak to the sons of Israel, saying,
> 'On the fifteenth of this seventh
> month is the Feast of Booths for
> seven days to the LORD. On the first
> day is a holy convocation; you shall
> do no laborious work of any kind.

48. leavened products containing yeast

49. seed, grape, fig, pomegranate, and olive

53

For **seven days** you shall present an offering by fire to the LORD. On the **eighth day** you shall have a holy convocation and present an offering by fire to the LORD; it is an assembly. You shall do no laborious work.

The graph below demonstrates the chiasm:

Bookend Overview:
Leviticus 23:1-2

↓

Commandments of Sukkot:
Leviticus 23:34-36

↑

Bookend Summary:
Leviticus 23: 37-38

Leviticus 23:1-2 summarizes what follows. Verses 37-38 provide a review of everything preceding it. Together they are the bookends of the feasts.

These are the appointed times of the LORD which you shall proclaim as holy convocations, to present offerings by fire to the LORD— burnt offerings and **grain offerings, sacrifices and drink offerings**, each day's matter on its own day besides those of the sabbaths of the LORD, and **besides your gifts and besides all your votive and freewill offerings**, which you give to the LORD. (Le 23: 37-38)

Inexplicably, although already described within the bookends, the text of Leviticus 23:39-43 continues to describe the seven days of Sukkot in detail without the eighth day included in the celebration *except as a day of rest*:

> On exactly the fifteenth day of the seventh month, when you have gathered in the crops of the land, you shall celebrate the feast of the LORD for **seven days**, with a rest on the first day and a rest on **the eighth day**. Now on the first day you shall take for yourselves the foliage of beautiful trees, palm branches and boughs of leafy trees and willows of the brook, and you shall rejoice before the LORD your God for **seven days**.
>
> **You shall thus celebrate it as a feast to the LORD for seven days in the year**. It shall be a perpetual statute throughout your generations; you shall celebrate it in the seventh month. **You shall live in booths for seven days**; all the native-born in Israel shall live in booths, so that your generations may know that I had the sons of Israel live in booths when I brought them out from the land of Egypt. I am the LORD your God. [50]

So is it a seven-day feast or an eight-day feast? Does the Eighth Day stand alone? If so, how can it be called The Eighth, for there is no eight without a seven. The hint is clear, but its meaning is not! If Moses is the prophecy, and the Prophets are his legs, the Prophet Chaggai may clarify it. Chaggai Two prophesies of a type of Sukkot beginning in the month of Kislev, but it is concealed to his generations.

50. Le 23:-39-43

55

Although modern Bibles have artificial chapters and verses inserted to improve readability, the ancient text did not. Immediately following the final instructions for the celebration of Sukkot in Leviticus 23, the text begins describing the service of the seven-branched golden menorah in the Tabernacle as "a law for the ages, throughout all your generations" (24:1 Schocken Bible Vol. 1). Textually, the seven/eight-day celebration of Sukkot is linked to the mysterious menorah.

The eighth day circumcision[51] implies that the eighth day transcends the created physical world of seven days. The completion of those seven days is the preparation for the eighth day. Because it transcends the physical world, the eighth has a hidden quality to it. God's people are aware of it, but they cannot fully engage it *before* the completed preparation of the seven days and Shabbat. A baby boy must have entered into a Shabbat before his physical circumcision on the eighth day. Circumcision is a required component of life in the Eighth Day.

51. the veil of skin or flesh removed in order to comprehend the spiritual

7

CHAGGAI AND CHANUKKAH ROOTS

*And the elders of the Jews were successful **in building** through the prophesying of Haggai the prophet and Zechariah the son of Iddo. And they finished building according to the command of the God of Israel and the decree of Cyrus, Darius, and Artaxerxes king of Persia.[52]*

The Eight-day celebration of Chanukkah is not exactly a *moed*; it is a rabbinic enactment commemorating an ancient miracle of deliverance from an abomination that caused desolation. That abomination was the offering of a pig on the Temple Mount by Antiochus Epiphanes, a Greek ruler succeeding Alexander the Great. Antiochus also erected Greek gods on the Mount. The Prophet Daniel predicted this abomination that caused desolation as well as the correct sequence of conquering kingdoms.

Chanukkah is celebrated and commemorated for eight days as a minor holiday for Orthodox Jews around the world. It is not celebrated as equal with a *moed* (feast) of High Sabbath; however, like Purim

52. Ez 6:14

in the Book of Esther, there is no work proscription. There are seven days of the year on which Israelites are prohibited from working: the first and last days of Passover and Sukkot, Shavuot, Rosh Hashanah, and Yom Kippur.

Another word for holiday or celebration is *chag*, and it usually refers to the three pilgrimage feasts of Passover, Shavuot (Pentecost or Weeks), and Sukkot, so a chag and moed are similar, yet not exactly the same. The ancient root *chagag* means to celebrate, stagger, or reel about in a circle. In this respect, it is like the appointed feasts that also move in a circuit annually. Yom Kippur, however, is a moed, yet it is not distinguished by eating, drinking, and joyful celebration, but by the affliction of the soul on that day.

The prophet Haggai prophesies of the inauguration of a blessing on the products that characterize the celebration of Sukkot. Haggai's Hebrew name is *Chaggai*, in which one can hear the same root as *chag*, or festive celebration. His name means "My feast." Among all the scholars and prophets who returned from Babylon to rebuild Jerusalem, Chaggai's name hints that his prophecies will include information about Israel's past and future celebrations.

Chaggai's clue is in his prophecy concerning a blessing of Sukkot products that will begin on the 24th of Kislev. The only Jewish celebration that fits his precisely-timed prophecy is Chanukkah. The root of Chanukkah, *chanakh*, means dedication.

> **2596. chanak**; verb from 2441; to train up, dedicate

> **2598. chanukkah**; noun from the same as 2441; dedication, consecration (Thomas, 1998)

The First Mention[53] in Scripture of the verb root *chanakh* is in Deuteronomy 20:5 amid a chapter concerning war and rules of engagement. Significantly, the verse mentions a man's "house":

> The officers also shall speak to the people, saying, 'Who is the man that has built a new **house** and has not **dedicated** it? Let him depart and return to his house, otherwise he might die in the battle and another man would **dedicate** it.'

Of primary interest is the use of the word "house," which later was inaugurated as an idiom for The Temple in King Solomon's dedication prayer[54] for the Temple.

House = Temple

Past and future verb forms of chanakh are used in Verse Five: *chanakho* (dedicated), *yachnekhenu* (will dedicate). Because a certain man didn't dedicate it (past), another man will dedicate it (future). This hint is repeated in Haggai's prophecy on the 24th of Kislev concerning something that *will happen* on the 25th of Kislev, which is the first day of Chanukkah. This blessing that *will begin* on the 25th, Chaggai prophesies, is connected to an event that happened *in the past*.

> Set now your heart **from this day and before, from the twenty-fourth of the ninth month, back to the day when the foundations of the Sanctuary were laid**; set your heart: is there any more seed in the silo? Even the grapevine and the fig tree and the pomegranate tree and the olive tree have not borne their fruit. **But from this day on** I will provide blessing.[55]

53. The first use of the word (Rule of First Mention) in the Bible may hold a key to defining the word that will hold true through the Bible. If you see a consistent use and definition of a word that holds true through most of the text, then you have a good definition or interpretation. This is one of the rules of Hermeneutics, or methods of Biblical interpretation.

54. 1 Ki 8:12

55. Haggai 2:18

Chaggai's prophecy is that the blessing will be inaugurated on the 24th/25th[56] of the Ninth Month (Kislev) based on the previous establishment of the Temple. Two events marked the building of the House. First, a foundation is laid, and upon completion, the House is dedicated.

The foundation of the Temple was laid by Solomon one month after Passover in the second month Ziv,[57] which means "brilliance, splendor." The Torah records another discussion of something that can occur one month after the Passover:

> Speak to the sons of Israel, saying, 'If any one of you or of your generations becomes unclean *because of a dead person, or is on a distant journey,* he may, however, observe the Passover to the LORD. In the second month on the fourteenth day at twilight, they shall observe it; they shall eat it with unleavened bread and bitter herbs. They shall leave none of it until morning, nor break a bone of it; according to all the statute of the Passover they shall observe it.'[58]

In summary, if a person is unable to observe the first Passover because he has touched a corpse or has been on a far journey, then he is able to make up the feast one month later in the month of Ziv. [59] As seen with Solomon, this "foundation" of the House is built in Numbers Nine, which connects the foundation of the Temple in the second month of Ziv to the Passover in the first month, Nissan 15, by the question of ritual uncleanness to participate.

Chanukkah, however, was instituted in part because of missing Sukkot,[60] not Passover. By applying the "sheni" principle in Numbers after the war with the Greeks, the priests take a year (instead of a month[61]

56. Because the Biblical day is reckoned from the evening until the next evening, the modern Gregorian day of the 24th overlaps the 25th from evening until midnight. The Gregorian solar and Jewish lunar/ solar calendars are reckoned differently, so the days of the month will not be the same from year to year. See Kisha Gallagher's *BEKY Book The Biblical New Moon: A Guide to Celebrating* for additional information.

57. 1 Ki 6:1, 37-38

58. Nu 9:10-12

59. See Appendix E

60. 2 Maccabees 1:18

61. Gemara to Shabbat 21B

to cleanse the House and establish a makeup feast session to rededicate both the people and the House of God. It takes much longer to cleanse a House for an entire nation at Sukkot than to clean a single individual's house, but this may not be the only reason.

Another reason may be that the Torah uses particular wording contrasting Nisan, the month of Passover, and the fall feasts of Trumpets, Atonement, and Tabernacles. While Nisan is identified as the "beginning of the months," the fall feasts are identified as the "going out" of the year and the "turn" of the year.[62] The wording is not an accident, but likely part of a paradigm difficult for the "either/or" Western mindset to grasp. For the priests to wait a year for a sheni Sukkot instead of a month for a sheni Pesach makes contextual sense.

Chanukkah prayers mention two miracles: victory in war and the kindling of the lights in the Temple. The basis for the tradition of Chanukkah is first recorded in the Gemara to Shabbat 21b, which cites "thanks and praise," also a part of Sukkot celebration.

These are two seed thoughts from the Torah: the dedication of a house if one is engaged in a war and a "makeup session" of the celebration. The Israelite warriors had to "return" to the House from battle after being reminded by the priests and officers of their priority. Perhaps Adonai was telling the Israelites that attention to the House was the key to defeating any enemy!

In a spiritual sense, if there was no return (repentance), then an idolatrous worship system could take possession of the Temple. The Greeks did this with their idols in the Temple until the officers of the Maccabees and other heroes, such as Channah and her seven sons,[63] inspired the Jews to repent and let Adonai fight for them. In fact, this reminder that the God of Israel would fight for them preceded

62. See BEKY Booklet *Truth, Tradition, or Tare?: Growing in the Word* pages 55-56 for examples of the fall feasts' thematic connection to years in the Torah.

63. Read the books of the Maccabees for this and other stories of heroism.

the reminder concerning dedication of the house in Deuteronomy 20.

Additionally, if a soldier had betrothed a virgin and not married her, he was to return to marry her lest another man take his place if he died in war. Once he marries her, Torah enjoins upon any soldier the obligation of staying home to make her happy for one year before he can return to the battle.[64] Both the dedication of Solomon's Temple and the re-dedication of the Temple under the Hasmoneans involved a one-year delay[65] from completion until the dedication ceremony. Might we celebrate a "happy millennium" with our Messiah before the final battle prophesied in Revelation when the Enemy is once again loosed to deceive mankind?

A man who refuses to dedicate his house or marry his betrothed is a man without faith. He is planning to die! This is not the kind of soldier who can be used of *Adonai Tzvaot* in a battle, especially since he's been advised that the battle is not his, but Adonai's. Such a man does not believe that Adonai will defeat the enemy. It is the job of the priests and officers to ensure that every man has faith in the power of The Holy One to defeat the Wicked One. Otherwise, he is unsuited for battle. He should *shuv* (return) and repent of his faithlessness by dedicating his house and marrying. He should believe in Moses and the Prophets.

In the war against the Greeks, Judah Maccabee followed this instruction of the Torah by sending home the newlyweds:

> Then they sounded the trumpets and gave a loud shout. After this Judas appointed leaders of the people, in charge of thousands and hundreds and fifties and tens. *Those who were building houses, or were about to be married, or were planting a*

64. Dt 24:5

65. Gemara to Shabbat 21b

vineyard, or were fainthearted, he
told to go home again, according
to the law. Then the army marched
out and encamped to the south of
Emmaus.[66]

What followed Judas' act of obedient faith was one
of the greatest defeats of the Greeks in war. The
Greeks fled in total terror from only three thousand
Jewish warriors.

The human being in fear of war and destruction is the
vital component of dedication. After all, if a man set
out to battle without dedicating his house, then his
unspoken plan was for failure and destruction. Why
bother to dedicate what another man would take?
This echoes Esau's musing that the birthright would
do him no good considering he was going to die. He
didn't mean literally die, for food was accessible in
the camp. Esau acknowledged that the benefits of
the birthright would only be realized many hundreds
of generations after his death. Why bother?

Rabbi Fohrman reminds his listeners concerning
Chanukkah, "People were responsible for bringing
light back into the world." (Fohrman, 2016) When
the Israelite soldier initiated the steps of return (shuv),
the Holy One responded to the soldier's initiative by
giving the victory. Likewise, by the Jews' initiative in
returning (shuv) to the faith of their fathers, a faith
untainted by assimilation into an idolatrous and anti-
Torah culture, the Holy One responded by providing
the miraculous oil.

Rabbi Fohrman (ibid) suggests that while Adam
and the idolators' winter solstice celebrations
commemorate the "revival of God's light in nature,"
the Jews' Chanukkah celebration commemorates
the "revival of God's light in history...and human
affairs." He further elaborates, "If we feel that God
is leaving us, we need to actually take action...we
can't wait for light to arrive to reassure us that God is

66. 1 Mac
3:54–57

63

here...if we want God to be here, we need to invite Him back."

Instead of eulogizing and celebrating only the God of nature and His natural order of things that moves in cycles regardless of man's sin, human beings must initiate a return to the House and celebrate the Creator's miraculous intervention in the new dedication. God is willing to suspend the laws of nature when mankind returns his heart to the House of worship.

Another Torah Seed commandment that hints to a time when additional lights will be lit is found in Leviticus:

> Command the sons of Israel that
> they bring to you clear oil from
> beaten olives for the light, to make
> **a lamp** burn continually. Outside
> the veil of testimony in the tent of
> meeting, Aaron shall keep it in order
> from evening to morning before
> the LORD continually; it shall be
> a perpetual statute throughout
> your generations. He shall keep
> **the lamps** in order on the pure
> gold lampstand before the LORD
> continually.[67]

Within the same text, the menorah is referred to both as the lamp, singular, and the lamps, plural. Judaism sees this text as a possible seed or hint to the chanukkiah, and it follows on the puzzling chapter describing both a seven and eight-day celebration of Sukkot.

After seven years of building, Solomon's Temple was completed in the Eighth Month, the month of Bul, which like the makeup session of Passover (*Pesach Sheni*), is one month after Sukkot. King Solomon, the priests, and Levites take a year to prepare, and then

67. Le 24:2–4

they dedicate the Temple at Sukkot in the Seventh Month.[68] The Hebrew text of 1 Kings 8:63 elucidates important themes: the House, dedication, the king, the children of Israel.

> **Vah-yahchnekhu et-beit Yehovah ha-melekh veh-khol-bnei Yisrael.**
>
> **And dedicated the House of Yehovah the King and all the children of Israel.**

As told to Chaggai, something that *has happened* in the House is the foundation of what *will happen* on Kislev 24/25. The foundation of the House was laid in the month of Ziv (Pesach Sheni for a corpse). The completion of the House was in the month of Bul (Sukkot Sheni). The first dedication of the House was a doubled Sukkot of fourteen days plus one day: the Eighth Day, or Shemini Atzeret. Even the products mentioned in Chaggai's prophecy of Chapter Two are specifically products offered at Sukkot: grain, grape, fig, pomegranate and olive.

Although Rambam in *Beis HaBechirah* wrote that Solomon's dedication is effective eternally (Scherman & Zlotowitz, Ed., 1990, p. 199), the Talmud (Shevuos 16a) records that the Babylonian destruction ended it. For Chaggai, the first House dedication was significant. Upon their return from Babylon, the men of the Great Assembly[69] rededicated the second Temple at the time of the completion of Jerusalem's rebuilt city walls. The rebuilding and rededication was after the Jews returned from Babylon under Ezra and Nehemiah, and Chaggai was one of the men of

68. 1 Ki 8:1-5. The text calls the Seventh Month *Eitanim*, but it also goes by the name Tishrei. Eitanim alludes to the rains that begin to fall in the Seventh Month, but Tishrei alludes to its position as head of the year, for in this month are the Jubilee Year and Shmittah Years proclaimed.

69. See S. Creeger's BEKY Book *Introduction to the Jewish Sources* for a review of the Men of the Great Assembly.

this Great Assembly.

The post-exilic rededication of the Sanctuary of the House coincides with the consecration of the rebuilt city walls of Jerusalem (ibid, p. 208). The Book of Nehemiah (12:27, 37-38) records:

> At the **dedication** (*chanukkat*) of the wall of Jerusalem, the Levites were sought from all their places to be brought to Jerusalem to perform the **dedication** (*chanukkah*) with rejoicing..."

> Then, before the Gate of the Spring; they ascended further to the steps of the City of David until the Water Gate to the east. Now the **second thanksgiving** went alongside..." (Artscroll Tanach, Stone Edition)

Two important themes are connected with this feast of dedication: water and thanksgiving. As the Gemara comments to Shabbat 21b, thanks and praise are the basis for observing Chanukkah. "The songs of praise and thanks" are detailed as part of the processional in Nehemiah 12:46.

Jewish tradition hands down water themes during Sukkot as well. The world is judged for rain at Sukkot,[70] and the Second Temple era celebrated a water-pouring ceremony each Sukkot. Notably, Yeshua stood up in the Temple at the time of the water-pouring ceremony at Sukkot and identified himself with the ritual.[71]

Associated with the water and thanksgiving offering in Nehemiah's procession is another appearance of something doubled, the *Todah Shenit*, or Second Thanksgiving. Collectively, foundation building and dedication ceremonies include months or celebrations of:

70. Chaggai 1:10

71. Jn 7:37-38

66

Passover Sheni	Second Passover
Sukkot Sheni	Second Tabernacles
Toda Shenit	Second Thanksgiving Offering
Doubled Sukkot (14 days)	Two Tabernacles

Having a double or repeat of something implies that the first existed. Two Passovers. Two thanksgiving offerings. Two Sukkot weeks. One-two. The Hebrew letter representing the number two is *beit*, which literally means a house. The Hebrew letters that spell Av are *alef-beit*, which numerically represent 1-2. The month of Av is the chiastic axis (middle month) between Passover and Chanukkah. In other words, because it is the axis between Passover and Chanukkah, then both will have a 1-2 theme.

Chaggai's prophecy consists of:

> Chapter 1:1-2 First prophecy comes exactly one month before Rosh HaShanah (Feast of Trumpets). It commands the (re)building of the Second Temple.

> 1:3-11 The "Chanukkah" prophecy gives Sukkot feast coordinates to Chaggai: sowing, reaping, drinking, dressing, carrying money, produce, grain, wine, oil, animal.

The specific mentions of sowing, reaping, produce, grain, wine, oil, and animal allude to the Sukkot sacrifices. Drinking alludes both to the commandment to drink in thanksgiving at Sukkot as well as to the traditional Jewish water theme of Sukkot and the "Last Great Day." Dressing alludes to the new clothes that traditionally are worn at Rosh HaShanah. Carrying money is part of Sukkot, for produce or animals may be sold for money to carry to Jerusalem to purchase sacrifices, drinks and foods to celebrate the feast. All these Sukkot themes are the roots of Sukkot in Chanukkah.

8

TWO MESSIAHS? A PARABLE

A parable in Scripture is a *mashal*. The Book of Proverbs according to its name in the Hebrew Bible is *Mishlei*, "The Parables of." Although couched in wisdom literature, the Book of Proverbs is parables of the Holy Spirit epitomized by the Woman of Valor and its antithesis The Adulteress. On the exterior, they are remarkably similar,[72] for they dress similarly, sit in the same places, prepare food and drink, and call to the same people. The vital difference, however, is that the harlot has "forgotten the covenant of her youth." In other words, she has departed from the Word of God.

Such parables and metaphors, said the great Jewish scholar Rambam, are the key to understanding the Scriptures (Mitchell, 2016, p. 25). Indeed, Yeshua relied heavily on parables to make his points. Parables are used when it is difficult for human beings to grasp spiritual concepts, so they are dressed in human clothes to aid understanding. Both the Book of Proverbs and the Gospels are full of parables contrasting the wise to the fool.

In careful analysis, like the courageous woman and adulteress of Proverbs, the characters in the parables

72. See Creation Gospel Workbook Four: *the Scarlet Harlot and the Crimson Thread* for a full explanation of these two types from Genesis to Revelation.

exhibit similar characteristics. Both the faithful wife and the adulteress are women. Correspondingly, both the wise man and the fool are men. It is their choices relative to the parable that prove the intrinsic character of the individual man or woman. As with the supernatural fire pattern (see Appendix B), the differences between life and destruction are not always Israel vs Foreign Enemy, but sometimes Israel vs Apostate Israel, the enemy within who appears to be a brother.

A contranym in Scripture is a word or concept that represents two sides or possibilities within the same person or concept. For instance, the English word "cleave" can mean both to cut in two pieces or to cling tightly. A human being is also a contranym, for by choice, a human being can depart from his Creator in rebellion or cling tightly to Him in obedience. Even the Apostle Paul lamented in the letter to the Romans that being a human meant to have a part of him who identified with the Torah (Law) instructions of Messiah and a part of him who wrestled with it.

Similarly, one human being may receive a blessing that requires two similar, yet very different, fulfillments. For instance, Judah's blessing was to be both a lion that no one dared to rouse, yet a humble donkey that was so tame it could be tied to the most tender of vines.[73] Joseph, too, received a blessing[74] that was even more stark in its contrast despite the similarity between the two symbols: the firstborn *shor* (domestic bull) and the *rem* (wild bull).

The *shor* was a tame animal born for the plow, food, or sacrifice. It was expected that the domestic shor was well-trained not to gore humans or to wander away habitually. A firstborn shor, however, was born to be a bloody sacrifice in the House.[75]

The *rem*, however, was a wild animal somewhat taller than a moose; it is called an *auroch* in English.

73. Ge 49:8-12

74. Dt 33:17

75. Nu 18:17

Even though the rem had the appearance and shape of a bull, it was not used for sacrifice, for it was a dangerous creature of epic size, speed, and fierceness. It stood nearly 6 1/2 feet tall at the shoulder, and it had huge horns that rose up to nine feet from the ground.

The auroch became extinct, and the last known auroch died in Poland in 1627. Ancient Roman history records the immense size of the animal, and its image adorned the Babylonian Ishtar Gate. In Scripture, Balaam spoke of its majesty in Numbers 23:22, and in Job 39:9-12, even The Holy One admires His work in creating the *rem*.

Although cousins, the shor and the rem were remarkably different animals, each representing an aspect of Joseph's blessing. As a metaphorical firstborn shor, Joseph's descendant was destined to die a bloody, humble sacrificial death for the family of Jacob. As the wild rem, though, Joseph's descendant would be a fierce warrior who gored and pushed the nations to the ends of the earth. "One is lowly and bound to slaughter. The other is sovereign and bound to life." (Mitchell, p. 22). From these metaphors, a rabbinic expectation of two messiahs emerged: Messiah ben Joseph by the way of the Suffering Servant and Messiah ben David as Conquering King.

Mitchell cites Genesis Rabbah 39.11, which gives a *mashal* (parable) to illustrate the two aspects that Jews believed characterized the coming Messiah. In the Genesis midrash, four types of "coins" are given as examples. A coin is one object, yet it has two sides; it is a contranym. In summary, the coins are:

- Abraham and Sarah. One side had the images of an old man and old woman, and on the other side the images of a youth and maiden. Through supernatural intervention, the old age of Abraham and Sarah became the youth of child-bearing age.

- Joshua (Yehoshua, the longer form of Yeshua). On one side of the coin was a firstborn shor, and on the other side the rem. The midrash points out that Joshua's fame was IN all the land. His humble service to Moses *outside* the Land is transformed to heroic military conquest IN the Land of Israel. He was from the tribe of Ephraim.

- David. A humble shepherd's staff and bag on one side, and a tower fortress on the other. The midrash says that David's fame went out into ALL the lands.

- Mordecai. Sackcloth and ashes on one side, and a golden crown on the other side. Mordecai's fame was both in the king's house and all the provinces. There were 127 provinces in the Persian kingdom, and Sarah died at age 127.

What can this parable teach about the Jewish expectations of Messiah?

First, his inclusive work is founded on the promise given to Abraham and Sarah to inherit a Land of Promise and become a great nation as well as to be the mother and father of many nations; this promise was given *before* the twelve tribes existed. Second, like Yehoshua the Ephraimite, the Messiah would be famous within the Land of Israel, conquering the idolatrous "seven nations" who were foreigners in the Land as well as purging those who were brothers straying from the covenant.[76] Yehoshua[77] married Rahab, a foreigner from *within* the Land promised to Israel. Third, like David the Jew, the Messiah's fame would extend into all the lands. He would be both a Shepherd and a warrior, rallying all Israel to him as the Lion of Judah.

76. Joshua 7:21-22

77. Mitchell points out (p. 24) that the Prophet Habakkuk presents Yehoshua (Joshua) as both the one for whom the sun and moon stood still (3:11) and "your Messiah" (3:12), or meshichekha; therefore the Yehoshua who succeeded Moses was an instrument of salvation (yeshuah) (3:8). Yeshua's role as Messiah (Mashiach) deliverer and salvation is established from the foundation of Yehoshua's leadership, yet Habakkuk prophesies of end time events. Yeshua's arrival as a warrior-prince like Yehoshua is part of Mashiach's second aspect, the rem.

Fourth, like Mordecai the Benjaminite in captivity in Babylon, Messiah would teach righteousness through humility and royal authority. He would bring the promise to Sarah full circle, drawing people to identify with the Jewish people from 127 provinces of the earth. Sarah died at age 127. The former poor orphan Esther became the blessing mother to many peoples in the kingdom. The Book of Revelation, like the Book of Esther, mentions people who call themselves Jews but are not. In a strange twist of history, tables are turned. In Esther 8:17, many were so awed by the power of the God of Abraham, Isaac, and Jacob that they became Jews.

In the Book of Revelation, those who call themselves Jews, but are not, will bow and admit that Yeshua loves the peoples from every nation, tribe, and tongue. Contextually, these loved people are children of the Valorous Woman Israel in Revelation, keeping the testimony of Yeshua and the commandments of God. They are part of the one flock of the Great Shepherd of the Sheep.

Historically, those who would have denied the non-Jew a place in the World to Come were Pharisees from the School of Shammai. It was the Pharisees from the School of Hillel who would welcome the converts from the nations and teach them God's Word. This is another example of those who are from among Israel, yet who are very different. Yeshua severely reprimanded his brothers from the School of Shammai for their harsh rulings.

If they had been Jews at heart, the Shammaites would have applied mercy in their applications of the Torah both on the native-born Israelite as well as the stranger coming to their gates to join them. They would have sought the rich inheritance of the four-point parables exemplified by their forefathers in faith, Abraham and Sarah, Joshua, David, and Mordecai. Their pattern was to gather the faithful from both the Land of Israel as well as the nations who began with no known Israelite tribal membership.

These two messianic characters, the suffering servant and conquering king who gathers and shepherds from both inside and outside the Land do not have to be two separate people. In a parable, the same person can have two aspects. The same Joseph who suffered at the hands of his estranged brothers and the Egyptians is the same Joseph who ruled as second to Pharaoh and reunited his brothers and the people of the land. The difficulty in reconciling the two aspects of Joseph explains the difficulty that is experienced when Yeshua walks in the Temple at Chanukkah in the Gospel of John.

> Have this attitude in yourselves
> which was also in Christ Jesus, who,
> although He existed in the form of
> God, did not regard equality with
> God a thing to be grasped, but
> emptied Himself, taking the form of
> a bond-servant, and being made in
> the likeness of men. Being found in
> appearance as a man, He humbled
> Himself by becoming obedient to
> the point of death, even death on
> a cross. For this reason also, God
> highly exalted Him, and bestowed
> on Him the name which is above
> every name, so that at the name of
> Jesus EVERY KNEE WILL BOW, of those
> who are in heaven and on earth
> and under the earth, and that every
> tongue will confess that Jesus Christ is
> Lord, to the glory of God the Father.
> [78]

The pattern of four contranym "coins" discussed earlier suggests three types of people incorporated into the Kingdom: the righteous native-born Israelite, 78. Phillipians the righteous stranger "within the gates" of Israel, 2:5–11 and those righteous among the nations who have no *known* pedigree as Israelite.

The prototypical couple Abraham and Sarah fit all three categories. They were called from Ur, outside the Land of Israel; they were justified in righteousness by their faith. They made a journey to the Land and dwelled there, growing in righteousness and faith. Later they journeyed to Egypt and then back to the Promised Land, entering again. This last time they conceived Isaac, who would father Jacob (Israel), establishing the bloodline of Israel. By this example, Paul explains to Gentiles that they are yet children of Abraham even without a Jewish pedigree, for like their father Abraham, they were called from the nations because of their faith.

The three angels who told Abraham and Sarah that they would conceive a son leave a clue in their visit to the righteous couple:

> So Abraham hurried into the tent to Sarah, and said, 'Quickly, prepare **three measures** (*seh-im*) of fine flour, knead *it* and make bread cakes.' [79]

Sarah was in her tent, hidden from view. In spite of this, the three angels heard her laugh! The rabbis write that this was supernatural hearing because Sarah laughed *within herself*, not audibly. She is having an internal conversation as she listens to the visitors speak with Abraham.

The context of this visit is the time of Passover, a week when no leaven can be used. Although one might say that before the giving of the Torah to Israel at Mount Sinai, no one knew the Law, there is evidence of people knowing and keeping many commandments of the Torah prior to that. As the angels move on to visit Lot in Sodom, he bakes for them *matzah*, or unleavened bread. Since Sarah was told to hurry, she would have baked matzah.

79. Ge 18:6

Traditionally, Isaac's birth is placed during Passover, for the angels tell Abraham that at the same time in the next year they would have the promised son. The *Targum*, an Aramaic explanation of the Hebrew Torah, contains the traditional insight as translated into English from Genesis 18:

> And the angels, who had the
> likeness of men, arose from thence,
> and the one who had made known
> the tidings to Sarah ascended to
> the high heavens; and two of them
> looked toward Sedom;

One of the angels is identified as YHVH,[80] and He is the Angel with whom Abraham bargains for Sodom. Only two angels move on to judge Sodom and Gomorrah. The one who delivers the Good News to Sarah ascends to Heaven and is hidden. One angel delivers Lot, a man called righteous because his soul was vexed by the wickedness of Sodom, yet he chose to mix himself there. He had the same familial bloodline as Abraham, yet he chose the benefits of the Sodomite economy. The last angel destroys all the wicked within Sodom.

The encounter transmits three types:

- Abraham and Sarah, righteous people who "made souls,"[81] or made converts to El Shaddai, even in Haran. They were being purified in holiness, yet they invited others in and became instruments of inclusion.

- Lot, a man relatively righteous, yet not holy because of his attachment to the benefits of the world. He was grieved by his lukewarm choice, but his redeeming virtue was hospitality and protection of strangers. Although of the bloodline of Abraham, he mixed himself with the nations.

80. the transliterated tetragrammaton of the holiest name of God, usually translated as Jehovah in English Bibles.

81. Ge 12:5

- The Sodomites, totally wicked, uninterested in repentance or hospitality of inclusion and protection of the vulnerable. The holy angels were supernaturally hidden from their sight even when the house was in plain sight.

Yeshua tells a very short parable to describe the Kingdom of Heaven in its fullness. He says,

> He spoke another parable to them,
> 'The kingdom of heaven is like
> leaven, which a woman took and
> hid in three pecks[82] of flour until it
> was all leavened.'[83]

The NASB Dictionary equates the Greek *saton* (peck) to the Hebrew *seah*. Additionally, the *Shem-Tov* Hebrew version of Matthew 13:33 specifically uses *se-im* (plural of seah) as the measure of flour. Yeshua intentionally uses the number and measure of Sarah's hidden flour.[84]

Although Sarah was asked to bake bread without leaven "quickly," Yeshua speaks of a woman who continues to hide the three measures of flour until it is completely leavened. The next *chag* after Passover is Shavuot (Pentecost), and two leavened loaves are offered. The final chag, however, is Sukkot, the Feast of the Nations. Leavened bread is enjoyed at Sukkot as well. Applying the Proverbs parable and metaphor of a "woman" as the Holy Spirit, it is the Holy Spirit that is working in concealment to leaven the dough of the whole Kingdom.

The middle feast of the three chagim (Passover, Shavuot, and Sukkot) is Shavuot, which literally means Weeks.[85] Apply the middle feast, Weeks, as the axis of the chiasm, and Shavuot's two leavened loaves represent two weeks, the week of Passover and the week of Sukkot.

82. Strong's #4568 saton; of Ara. or., cf. [5429]; seah, a (Heb.) measure.

83. Mt 13:33

84. Interestingly, flour offerings in the Torah come in measures of three-tenths!

85. Pentecost

Week of Passover

↑

Feast of Weeks -
Two Leavened Loaves

↓

Week of Sukkot

This leaven, however, is the leaven of the Kingdom, not sin. Leaven in Hebrew is *chametz*, which is a preservative. For instance, in Hebrew pickles are *chamutzim*, for the chametz of vinegar has preserved them from decay. The leaven of the Kingdom preserves living things, but the leaven of sin kills living things. Another contranym!

Here is a possible paradigm of the three feasts that "preserve" Israel:

86. Gerim in modern Jewish thought are full Jewish converts. See *Bnei Avraham Ahuvecha: gerim in Chassidic thought* by D. Ben Avraham for complete description. The convert Ruth is iconic of the Feast of Shavuot in Jewish thought, and the Book of Ruth is read in the synagogue.

- Passover represents the Israelites by blood who are obligated to the covenant of the Torah and first circumcision of the flesh.

- Shavuot represents the ger,[86] those proselytes of the gate who had gathered in Jerusalem in Acts Two; they were learning to obey Torah and were attracted to the Land and Israelite people. They were to become circumcised of flesh, their desire to cling to the Word and covenant People being evidence of a heart-first circumcision.

- Sukkot represents the inclusion of righteous Gentiles from among the nations who remain in place, yet worship monotheistically and keep many of the commandments given to Israel, such as the celebration of Sukkot and literally going up to Jerusalem at that time.[87] Paul suggests that these righteous Gentiles did not need physical circumcision, at least at that time. Circumcision was a requirement for fully obeying the commandments of Passover *in the Land*.

Because these three chagim represent the totality of the seven feasts and the fulfillment of a millennium of Sukkot, what lies beyond? Perhaps Methuselah prophesies of the Eighth Day, a Day when circumcision of both heart and flesh will be important. This will be explored in a later chapter.

> Peter said to Jesus, 'Rabbi, it is good for us to be here; let us make three tabernacles, one for You, and one for Moses, and one for Elijah.' For he did not know what to answer; for they became terrified. Then a cloud formed, overshadowing them, and a voice came out of the cloud, 'This is My beloved Son, listen to Him!' All at once they looked around and saw no one with them anymore, except Jesus alone.[88]

Think of the Prophet Micah's seven shepherds and eight leaders of men[89]. Moses preaches salvation to the Jew, the native-born Israelite; Elijah preaches salvation to the ger,[90] the stranger; and Yeshua is salvation to *both* the Jew and the Gentile. In one person, Yeshua is both the rem and the shor, both sides of the valuable coin of prophecy.

87. Zechariah 14

88. Mk 9:5-8

89. Micah 5:5

90. "But I say to you in truth, there were many widows in Israel in the days of Elijah, when the sky was shut up for three years and six months, when a great famine came over all the land; and yet Elijah was sent to none of them, but only to Zarephath, in the land of Sidon, to a woman who was a widow. And there were many lepers in Israel in the time of Elisha the prophet; and none of them was cleansed, but only Naaman the Syrian." (Lk 4:25–27)

79

TWIN PROPHETS

Among the converging themes of Chanukkah in the Torah and Prophets, there is a specific revisitation of the fall feast of Sukkot. The BEKY Booklet *Truth, Tradition, or Tare? Growing in the Word* includes a detailed discussion of how to distinguish Biblical truth from a tare of falsehood grown from a different seed. Additionally, the booklet helps readers differentiate between customs grown from the Biblical seed from traditions grown from or fused with the tare.

Jewish traditions are not necessarily an "addition to" the Torah. They were sprouted to bear fruit from the seed of the Torah text, not a new Torah. The fall feasts begin with the Feast of Trumpets:

> Speak to the sons of Israel, saying,
> 'In the seventh month on the first of
> the month you shall have a rest, a
> **reminder** by blowing of trumpets, a
> holy convocation.'[91]

Chanukkah sprouted from the fall feasts, which includes the Feast of Trumpets, Yom Kippur, and Sukkot. Zechariah was Chaggai's contemporary

91. Le 23:24

and his prophecy partner. The prophets Haggai and Zechariah prophesy of the inauguration of a blessing on the products characterizing the celebration of Sukkot. **Chaggai**'s name means "My feast." Zechariah means "Yah Remembers." Chaggai prophesies to *the Jews* about Israel's past and future celebrations. As a reminder, Chaggai prophesies to the Jews:

> So is this people and so is this nation before Me – the word of HaShem - and so is all their handiwork: what they offer there will be defiled... (2:14) ...Set now your heart from this day and before, from the twenty-fourth of the ninth month... (2:18) But from this day on I will provide blessing. (2:19) (Artscroll Stone Edition)

By directing Israelites to look back to the foundation of the First Temple on that day[92], the double Sukkot was brought to mind when the Hasmoneans cleansed the Temple. Chanukkah was observed as a Sukkot Sheni during the ninth month of Kislev.[93] The Temple had to be cleansed of the desecrations to the altar, so Sukkot in the 7th month could not be observed.

> Set now your heart from this day and before, from the twenty-fourth of the ninth month, *back to the day when the foundations of the Sanctuary were laid*; set your heart: is there any more seed in the silo? Even the grapevine and the fig tree and the pomegranate tree and the olive tree have not borne their fruit. But from this day on I will provide blessing."[94]

92. Hg 2:2-3

93. See Appendix C

94. Hg 2:18

A blessing will be inaugurated on the 24th/25th of the Ninth Month (Kislev) based on the previous establishment of the Temple. Zechariah echoes the prophecy of Chaggai by reminding Israel of the foundation of the First Temple:

> Thus says the LORD of hosts, 'Let your hands be strong, you who are listening in these days to these words from the mouth of the prophets, those who spoke in the day that the foundation of the house of the LORD of hosts was laid, **to the end** that the temple might be built.' [95]

Zechariah's prophecies of blessing parallel Chaggai's, but his prophecies expand from Judah to the nations. To the Jew, Zechariah encourages:

> Thus says the LORD of hosts, 'The fast of the fourth, the fast of the fifth, the fast of the seventh and the fast of the tenth months will become joy, gladness, and cheerful feasts *for the house of Judah*; so love truth and peace.'

To the stranger, Zechariah adds:

> Thus says the LORD of hosts, 'It will yet be that *peoples will come, even the inhabitants of many cities*. The inhabitants of one will go to another, saying, "'Let us go at once to entreat the favor of the LORD, and to seek the LORD of hosts; I will also go.'" *So many peoples and mighty nations will come to seek the LORD of hosts in Jerusalem* and to entreat the favor of the LORD. Thus says the LORD of hosts, '*In those days ten men from all the nations will grasp the garment of a Jew, saying, "'Let us go with you, for we have heard*

95. Zec 8:9

83

that God is with you.'"[96]

Zechariah continues prophesying, including the nations in a conditional blessing that at first was given only to the people Israel living in the Land of Israel. [97] The blessing for keeping covenant is rain on the Land. At that time, all nations who remain after the Holy One finally redeems the Land of Israel will come under the covenant condition. In prophesying the nations' desire to celebrate the Feasts of Israel, Zechariah specifically mentions Sukkot, the feast which Chaggai tied thematically to Chanukkah:

> Then it will come about that any who
> are left of *all the nations* that went
> against Jerusalem will go up from
> year to year to worship the King,
> the LORD of hosts, and to *celebrate
> the Feast of Booths.* And it will be
> that whichever of the families of the
> earth does not go up to Jerusalem to
> worship the King, the LORD of hosts,
> there will be no rain on them. If the
> family of Egypt does not go up or
> enter, *then no rain will fall on them*;
> it will be the plague with which the
> LORD smites the nations who do
> not go up to celebrate the Feast of
> Booths. *This will be the punishment
> of Egypt, and the punishment of all
> the nations who do not go up to
> celebrate the Feast of Booths.*[98]

Together, the twin prophets Chaggai and Zechariah give hope to the Jews returning from Babylon, but they also prophesy to those among the nations who will return with the Jew. Both are in need of rededication, and both will be rededicated through the work of the Seven Shepherds and the Eight Princes of men.

96. Zec 8:19-23

97. Le 26:4; Dt 11:14, 28:12

98. Zec 14:16-19

84

10

PRAY THAT YOUR FLIGHT BE NOT IN WINTER

The seven shepherds mentioned in the traditional Chanukkah liturgy are the key to unlocking Yeshua's role as the Shepherd of Israel. The Shepherd of Israel was prophesied by Ezekiel to increase the numbers of the flock called Israel:

> Thus saith the Lord GOD; I will yet for this be enquired of by the house of Israel, to do it for them; *I will increase them with men like a flock*. As the holy flock, as the flock of Jerusalem in her solemn feasts; so shall the waste cities be filled with flocks of men: and they shall know that I am the LORD.[99]

99. Ez 36:37-38

100. The Jewish sages volunteered an insight concerning why one increases the number of candles lit each night of Chanukkah: it represents the increasing number of bulls sacrificed at Sukkot on behalf of the nations.

Sukkot is called the Feast of the Nations because Zechariah envisions people from the nations identifying with that feast in particular.[100] Chanukkah, however, is a Sukkot Sheni, so why don't the nations identify with Chanukkah, only Jews? Most of the Jews of the 1st Century didn't want to wait for the Shepherd to increase the flock of men while they suffered at the hands of Rome, but perhaps today also there is a sense among sincere disciples of Yeshua that the celebration of Chanukkah is not needful. This could be a result of short-sighted vision and disregard for God-breathed prophecy.

Jews have owned the feast of Chanukkah throughout their generations, and likewise, Gentiles have rejected the feast as Jewish. With the wealth of Scriptures concerning the Sukkot Sheni of Chanukkah, however, the veil can only hang so long. Rather than attribute Jewish observance of Chanukkah to paganism and give a sneer at the pagan roots of Christmas, maybe there is a new way to think of both.

First, the early Christians were Jewish. They certainly understood the importance of Chanukkah in prophecy as Yeshua did. Even those who disbelieved Yeshua's messiahship knew enough to challenge him in the context of the Shepherd prophecy. Early believers would have celebrated Chanukkah with their Jewish brothers and sisters. Secondly, the Jewish apostles would have taught at least some of Chanukkah's importance to the Gentiles, at least until the Gentiles commandeered observance, including the Sabbath and feast days.

By the 3rd Century when the numbers of Gentiles overwhelmed those of Jewish believers, Chanukkah was replaced with a winter solstice celebration that included some pagan elements. Since the Roman calendar was solar, and the Jewish calendar lunar (with solar accommodations for the year and seasons), the month of Chanukkah was lost, but the date survived. Chanukkah will always begin on the 25th of Kislev on the Jewish calendar, but the date of the 25th will migrate through different dates on the Gregorian month of December, a solar calendar. With so many other things Jewish and Scriptural, the observance of Chanukkah was lost.

While certainly there was anti-Semitic and anti-rabbinic influence in the replacement of the Torah seed wheat with an unscriptural tare-tradition, not everyone who celebrated as a Christian did so with evil intent to change the times and seasons. "Never attribute to malice what is more properly attributable to ignorance."[101] As proof that the date still held a dim, if distant, connection to the Jewish celebration, the emblems of Sukkot still appear in Christmas celebrations: evergreen branches, lights, and sukkah (shelter hut where "Baby Jesus" slept).

It doesn't make sense that ill-informed lay Christians or even well-informed clerics would try to fuse Christmas with the actual time of Sukkot, which is in the fall season. If Sukkot Sheni, Chanukkah, was the actual date of remembrance, then it does make sense that they would retain the symbols. Off the mark, yes, but there was yet a memory of the importance of Chanukkah to the Gentiles. Not so coincidentally, the shepherds are the enduring visitors of Christmas stories.

The shepherds were witnesses to Yeshua's birth, which was likely during the fall feasts when the numbers of the flocks of men in Jerusalem would have swelled by over two million. For Joseph and Mary to find shelter in a rural sukkah in Bethlehem close to the holy city is logical. Fragments of the story recall other Chanukkah themes, such as the wise men following lights at night to reach the Redeemer of Israel. Like the noblemen who followed the High Priest all night with burning torches to avert the decreed destruction, so the wise men travelled by light not fueled by human hands.

Until Messiah returns to correct these mostly unintentional errors relative to His actual Word and commandments, there is one other way that the flocks of men can hear the voice of the Great Shepherd of the Sheep. Those who have accepted His Word can by example and their own words of

101. Hanlon's Razor

testimony return the vision of Chanukkah to the nations, for the righteous among the nations are equally invited to benefit from its prophetic blessing of Sukkot. Chaggai and Zechariah, and therefore the Holy One of Israel, said so.

While some may object, citing the numbers of those who would never exchange Christmas for a "Jewish" holiday, there are examples of such a paradigm shift. The mixed multitude of Egyptians left Egyptian gods and holidays; the people among the 127 Babylonian provinces who accepted the God of Israel under Queen Esther changed alliances, so there is hope. Faith in Yeshua is a great place to start walking toward full truth and Sukkot blessing.

SEVEN SHEPHERDS IN TRADITION

Here is a passage of remembrance from the Jewish liturgy that is prayed during Chanukkah:

> And for the miracles, the salvation, the mighty deeds, the victories, the wonders, the consolations, and for the battles which You performed for our fathers in those days, at this time...
>
> In the days of Mattisyahu, the son of Yochanan, the High Priest, the Hasmonean, and his sons when the wicked Greek kingdom rose up against Your people Israel to cause them to forget Your Torah and force them to stray from the statutes of Your Will. You in Your great mercy stood up for them in the time of their tribulation...
>
> You took up their grievance, judged their claim, and avenged their wrong. You delivered the strong

into the hands of the weak, the many into the hands of the few, **the impure** into the hands of the pure, **the wicked** into the hands of the righteous, and the cruel into the hands of the diligent disciples of Your Torah...

For Yourself You made a great and holy Name in Your world, and for Your people Israel You brought a great victory and *salvation*[102] at this very time. Then Your children came to the Holy of Holies of Your House, cleansed Your Temple, purified the place of Your holiness and kindled lights in the Courtyard of Your sanctuary;

They established these eight days of Chanukkah for thanks and praise to Your great Name.[103]

Bare Your holy arm and hasten the end for *salvation*. Avenge Your servant's blood from *the wicked* nation. For the victory is too long delayed for us, and there is no end to days of evil. *Repel the **Red One** in the farthest shadow and establish for us the **seven** shepherds*.[104]

The Seven Shepherds and the Red One are the missing Sukkot/Chanukkah links. In the Talmud, Jewish expectation concerning the Seven Shepherds and Eight Princes of men is given in a list. According

102. Yeshua's name means salvation

103. Shabbat Minchah as **extra** prayer of the **Modim** (double Thanksgiving) p. 567. Artscroll.

104. ibid, p. 833

to Jewish expectation, envision the following two lamps, one a seven-branched menorah, and one of eight branches (really nine).

On the seven-branched menorah:

- Adam, Seth and Methuselah [non-Jews] on his right
- David in the middle
- Abraham, Jacob and Moses [Jews] on his left.

| Abraham | Jacob | Moses | David | Methuselah | Seth | Adam |
| **Jews** | | | | | **Non-Jews** | |

On the eight branches:

> And who are the 'eight princes among men'? Jesse, Saul, Samuel, Amos, Zephaniah, Zedekiah, **the Messiah**, and Elijah.[105]

Jesse   Saul   Samuel   Amos   Zephaniah   Zedekiah   Elijah   Messiah

There are discrepancies in the ancient sources as to whether Messiah is seventh and Elijah eighth, or if Elijah is seventh and Messiah is eighth. This is not unusual, for even Yeshua made cryptic statements about Elijah. Had he already come, or was he coming? Yes, said Messiah in Matthew 17:11-12. This may allude to the prophetic pattern of Chaggai and Zechariah, and Yeshua spoke of things that had occurred in the past that were foundational to future expectation. The principle of consecutive numbers

105. The *Yalkut* and *Ein Jacob* have Elijah before Messiah. Sukkah 52b.

representing the physical leading to a more spiritual level is seen in the 7-8 shepherd-princes.

The Talmud connects Chanukkah's Seven Shepherds and Eight Princes with Sukkot laws, embedding Messiah as the 7th or 8th leader. Methuselah seems an odd choice as one of the Seven Shepherds, but he was the 8th generation from Adam. A list of seven ushpizin (guests at Sukkot)[106] teaches another aspect of Chanukkah; in some traditions, they are the Seven Shepherds:

> It is known that on the first night of Sukkot a mysterious guest sometimes appears in the booths of the righteous. This is none other than Abraham, who is the first of seven guests to appear, one on each night of the festival. On the second night Isaac appears, and on the third, Jacob. Joseph appears on the fourth night, Moses on the fifth, Aaron on the sixth, and King David on the last night of Sukkot. Blessed indeed, are those who receive these guests, who are known as the Seven Shepherds. Every day of Sukkot one of these seven shepherds arrives at the sukkah as a guest. (Schwarz, 2006, p. 299)

In the one reference to Chanukkah in the Book of John, "The Jews" ask Yeshua if he is the Messiah. David was the Seventh Shepherd, and Messiah would be Son of David, the Shepherd King. Apply the 1-2 principle, and the Seventh Shepherd is the physical descendent of David, but also the Eighth Prince, the Messiah anointed of the Holy Spirit.

The Eighth Shepherd-Prince would arrive at Chanukkah to deliver the Temple from the Romans, also known as Edom, who is called the Red One.

106. Eisenberg, 2010, pp. 235-236.

The Romans later literally placed another idol Abomination that Causes Desolation on the Temple Mount like the Greeks. Like Peter, the Jews expected a total deliverance and restoration of the Kingdom during their generation. Messiah the Shepherd was expected and prophesied to do this. Yeshua answered them,

> I told you, and you do not believe; the works that I do in My Father's name, these testify of Me. But you do not believe because you are not of **My sheep**. My **sheep** hear My voice, and I know them, and they follow Me; and I give eternal life to them, and they will never perish; and no one will snatch them out of My hand. My Father, who has given them to Me, is greater than all; and no one is able to snatch them out of the Father's hand. I and the Father are one.[107]

Chanukkah is a Sukkot Sheni. Because of the Roman defilement of the holy spaces and the priesthood, Jews were once again looking for the Seven Shepherds and the Eight Leaders of Men. The Eighth is Messiah, the Great Shepherd of the Sheep. Messiah, however, needed to account for Zechariah's prophecy of the nation-sheep, and Yeshua speaks of sheep who know his voice.

What follows is a very long summarizing quote, but context is needed for its themes: battle, shepherds, deliverance, recovering Israel from the nations, a Messiah:

> Now muster yourselves in troops, daughter of troops; they have laid siege against us; with a rod they will smite the judge of Israel on the cheek. But as for you, Bethlehem

107. Jn 10:22-30

92

Ephrathah, too little to be among
the clans of Judah, from you One will
go forth for Me to be ruler in Israel.
His goings forth are from long ago,
from the days of eternity. Therefore,
He will give them up until the time
when she who is in labor has borne
a child. Then the remainder of His
brethren will return to the sons of
Israel. And He will arise and shepherd
His flock in the strength of the LORD,
in the majesty of the name of the
LORD His God. And they will remain,
because at that time He will be
great to the ends of the earth.

This One will be our peace. When
the Assyrian invades our land, when
he tramples on our citadels, *then
we will raise against him Seven
shepherds and eight leaders of men.*
They will shepherd the land of Assyria
with the sword, the land of Nimrod
at its entrances; and He will deliver
us from the Assyrian when he attacks
our land and when he tramples our
territory. Then the remnant of Jacob
will be among many peoples like
dew from the LORD, like showers on
vegetation which do not wait for
man or delay for the sons of men.
[108]

The remnant of Jacob will be among many peoples...

This explains Yeshua's answer. The Jews expected
the Messiah to deliver them from wicked Rome like
Judah Maccabee delivered them from Greece. 108. Mic 5:1–8

Yeshua could not do it at that time because it did not allow for gathering the lost sheep. He did, however, *lay the foundation* of fulfilling the prophecies of Chaggai, Zechariah, and Micah to collect the sheep among the nations:

> I am the good shepherd, and I know
> My own and My own know Me, even
> as the Father knows Me and I know
> the Father; and I lay down My life for
> the sheep. I have other sheep, which
> are not of this fold...[109]

Chanukkah prayers mention two miracles: Victory in war and the kindling of the lights in the Temple. The holiday was set the following year for "thanks and praise," for the Greek army had destroyed all but one flask of oil when they invaded the Temple. Whether the continuously burning flame of the menorah celebrated by Chanukkah is truth or legend is not important; its connection to prior miracles is important, particularly the burning bush in Exodus 3:1-4.

Moses brought *the sheep* to the "mountain of God." An angel appears from the midst of the bush, but neither the bush nor the angel is consumed by the fire. God Himself calls to Moses from the midst of the bush. So who is the Angel in the bush other than Yeshua, the One sent from God? It was only when God saw that Moses turned and observed how remarkable was the miracle that He spoke to him. Moses was able to lead out of tribulation *both Israel and the mixed multitude of sheep.* On the other hand, many in Yeshua's day did not stop and consider the process of Messiah's work, nor its inclusiveness of the sheep among the nations. Yeshua's work is to bring *many sheep* to the mountain of God, the Torah.

> I am the good shepherd, and I know
> My own and My own know Me, even
> as the Father knows Me and I know

109. Jn 10:1-16

the Father; and I lay down My life for
the sheep. I have other sheep, which
are not of this fold...

I must bring them also, and they
will hear My voice; and *they
will become one flock with one
shepherd.*[110]

THE RED ONE AND THE BEAST

In the New Testament, there is only one other
mention of "winter" other than the mention of Yeshua
walking in the Temple at the Feast of Dedication,
Chanukkah. Words mean things, and so does their
placement. The winter celebration of Chanukkah
was significant in its placement in the Book of John,
not random. Likewise, the other mention of winter
in Matthew adds more context to the apocalyptic
Jewish expectations of Messiah.

> Therefore, when you see the
> ABOMINATION OF DESOLATION
> which was spoken of through Daniel
> the prophet, standing in the holy
> place (let the reader understand),
> then those who are in Judea must
> flee to the mountains...**But pray that
> your flight will not be in the winter, or
> on a Sabbath.**[111]

There are two times that Yeshua doesn't want his
sheep to take flight: winter or Shabbat. Jewish
liturgy gives the rationale. Every Shabbat, the Torah,
the covenant Word of God, is removed from the
ark and held up for the congregation to see. The
congregation responds with these words initiated by
Moses:

> Arise, O Lord, and *let Your enemies
> be scattered*; and let them who
> hate You flee from You. For from Zion

110. Jn 10:14–16

111. Mt 24:15–20

95

will go forth the Torah, and the Word
of the LORD from Jerusalem. Blessed
be He, Who in His holiness gave His
Torah to His people Israel.[112]

Those who flee and scatter from the Holy One on
Shabbat are His enemies! Shabbat is the Waterloo
of spiritual battles, for it is the eternal sign of betrothal
between the Holy One and Israel. The wicked are
destined to scatter on a great Shabbat to come.

Why not flee in winter? The only significant date
in winter is Chanukkah. The synagogue liturgy
reinforces the apocalyptic nature of the feast:

> Bare Your holy arm and hasten the
> end for salvation[113] - Avenge the
> vengeance of Your servant's blood
> from the wicked nation. For the
> triumph is too long delayed for us,
> and there is no end to days of evil.
> Repel the **Red One** in the nethermost
> shadow and establish for us the
> **seven** shepherds.[114]

112. Nu 10:35

113. Yeshua
means
"salvation"

114. Scherman,
1996, p. 833

115. See *Truth,
Tradition, or
Tare? Growing
in the Word* or
*Creation Gospel
Workbook
One* for a full
explanation of
Sardis as the
Feast of Trumpets

The siddur explains the key players of the
Chanukkah liturgy: "The **Red One** (*Admon*) refers
to Esau/Edom, whose descendants brought the
current exile. The **seven shepherds** of Micah 5:4
will conquer Israel's oppressors." (Scherman,
p. 832) Yeshua did not want his sheep to be
scattered on Chanukkah, for it would mean that
they were running from him, the Shepherd Prince!

The Feast of Trumpets (Rosh HaShanah) kicks off the
fall season of feasts that include Atonements and
Sukkot. Sardis, which represents Rosh HaShanah
in the Book of Revelation,[115] literally means "Red
Ones." Enemies scatter when the Torah goes forth on
Shabbat, and the Red Ones along with the Wicked
One are scattered in winter, Chanukkah.

The other mention of "winter" in the *Brit HaChadasha* (New Testament) was the inquiry addressed to Yeshua in the Temple.

> At that time the Feast of the Dedication took place at Jerusalem; **it was winter**, and Jesus was walking in the temple in the *portico of Solomon*. The Jews then gathered around Him, and were saying to Him, 'How long will You keep us in suspense? *If You are the Christ, tell us plainly*.' [116]

Solomon dedicated the First House, so it was no accident that Yeshua was questioned in the portico of Solomon. "The Jews" ask Yeshua if he is the 8th Shepherd Prince desired at Chanukkah to deliver the Temple from the Romans, Edom, the Red One, The Wicked, the Abomination that Causes Desolation. Because Messiah Son of David is the last of the seven shepherds, the Jews say that it is time for Yeshua to speak plainly...and he did!

Yeshua spoke of himself as the Shepherd calling sheep, but he says that the doubters cannot hear his voice. In the desire for short-term deliverance from Rome (also called Edom), the doubters had forgotten long-term salvation spoken of by the prophets in the context of the Seven Shepherds. Deliverance from the Red One is not merely deliverance from Rome or any other regime in a given generation, but deliverance from the Red One within the man that wars against the *Ruach Adonai* (Spirit of Adonai).

Apart from the Ruach, the man is nothing more than a human who conforms himself to the image of the beast-serpent, icons in Revelation that are familiar to Bible readers. Because Adam and Eve disregarded the Spirit of the commandment and conformed themselves to the soul-driven desires of the beast, they fell to their earthy, animal nature.

116. Jn 10:22–24

97

Without the Ruach, what differentiates a man from a beast? Such a man becomes a Red One, for his base substance was taken from the earth (*adamah*) like a beast, and the Hebrew root of earth is also the root of the color red (*adom*).

Like every human being who has ever lived, those who challenged Yeshua in the Temple at Chanukkah were looking for the "Red One" to be vanquished outside of themselves. If only Assyria, Babylon, Greece, or Rome could be vanquished... Those things, however, are outside the control of the individual. The Red One within *is* under control of the individual with the help of the Ruach HaKodesh, the Comforter sent from the Father.

The serpent-beast appeals to a human being at the level of his soul (appetite, emotion, desire, and intellect). He entices the soul to dominate the ruach within a man. If the serpent can seduce the man with his "red" desires to dominate the Ruach within, then the beast is the victor. The man's ruach, however, longs to connect with the Ruach HaKodesh, the Spirit of God that sets him apart from the animal kingdom. The evil inclination may be described as that animal soul striving against obedience to the spiritual commandments, for Paul writes that the Law is spiritual.[117]

If the Law and commandments are only the letter, then they are earthy. If they are engaged with the power of the Ruach HaKodesh, then they are spiritual and holy, as Paul writes. The letter is engaged with the short-sightedness of an animal. The spiritual commandment that gives life to the letter requires long-term vision. The Adversary's greatest weapon of temptation is to entice a human being into short-sighted benefits, just as he attempted to entice Yeshua during his forty days in the wilderness.

117. Ro 7:12 At the conclusion of the 7th "Day" millennium, John writes that the Adversary, who had been bound,

will be loosed again[118] to sift those unready for the Eighth Day Millennium. In Jewish tradition, the Adversary (satan) is the Yetzer Hara, the Evil Inclination. The Eighth Day requires the circumcision of spirit for survival, just as the first national celebration of Passover required circumcision of the flesh (Jo 5:5). Without circumcision of the Spirit, the Adversary can deceive with temptations to the soul and its covering veil of flesh.

A Jewish baby boy must be circumcised on the eighth day to remind him daily to engage the commandments of the covenant with long-term vision, that is, the Ruach HaKodesh. This is prophecy. The Covenant People desire resurrection of spirit, soul, and flesh. While the timing and dynamics of this transformation remain mysterious, these examples from the Word help the prophecy student to "flesh out" the full meaning of circumcision and the importance of the Eighth.

For example, Noah and his family were eight people. In their generation, the Creation fell to an inferior state, but eight people were saved by faith. When the Adversary has achieved his final deception of the "fallen" at the twilight of the Seventh Millennium and the dawn of the Eighth, a circumcised People will again be saved from destruction.

The difference is that instead of surviving to live in a fallen Creation, the resurrected righteous will live uprightly in an elevated dwelling place, untroubled further by the Adversary. A passage of the Jewish Blessing After Meals on Shabbat includes pleas for Adonai to

- Guide [walk] us upright [arisen] to our Land
- Cause us to inherit the day which will be total Shabbat and rest for all eternity

These Sabbath blessings anticipate that the full training program instituted by Messiah during the

118. Re 20

99

Seventh Millennium of Yom Shekulo Shabbat (a day that is all Shabbat) will fully tenderize resurrected hearts. These circumcised hearts will be upright and prepared for their Shabbat rest to extend into the Eighth Day and eternity.

Sukkah 52b records several names by which the Evil Inclination is known:

- The Enemy
- Stumblingblock
- Heart of Stone
- The Hidden One
- Unclean
- **The Uncircumcised**[119]

All through Scripture there are clues to the final battles for the hearts of human beings. The circumcision always has been a prophetic reminder to Israel that the world to come may only be engaged by those circumcised in heart and body. Like the resurrection that knits, forms, and fuses the spirit, soul, and body together, circumcision of the heart will be a final rejection of the Adversary, for the Eighth Day eternal circumcision of the stony heart is the sign of the New Covenant prophesied by Jeremiah 31:33 and Ezekiel 11:19-20.

On the eighth day, there is no requirement to dwell in sukkot, nor are ushpizin sent to judge the sukkah. What (or who) happens in the eighth generation?

The Seventh...no...the Eighth Shepherd of the Princes, the Prince of Peace, Yeshua returns. The Lion of the Tribe of Judah who said to his sheep, "If you love me, keep my commandments."

"THIS ONE will be our peace..."

119. See Appendix D

11

ENOCH, THE SEVENTH FROM ADAM

A Biblical figure whose name also means dedication is Enoch, or in Hebrew transliteration, *Chanokh*. Chanukkah is a feminine form of the root, and in Hebrew, the "spirit words" such as *Ruach* (Spirit), *Chokhmah* (Wisdom), *Binah* (Understanding), etc., are also feminine nouns. Chanukkah, a feminine noun, holds a spiritual hint in its connection to Chanokh, a man who walked so closely with God that "he was not, for he was taken." After all, Paul writes that the natural is revealed first, and then the spiritual.[120]

Is this winter celebration of dedication, Chanukkah, connected thematically to a human being so dedicated to his Creator that he disappeared? Yeshua spoke of a disappearance or "flight" in winter.

> **Jared lived** one hundred and sixty-two years, and became the father of Enoch. Then Jared lived eight hundred years after he became the father of Enoch, and he had other sons and daughters. So all the days of Jared were nine hundred

120. 1 Co 15:44-46

and sixty-two years, and he died. **Enoch lived** sixty-five years, and became the father of Methuselah. Then Enoch walked with God three hundred years after he became the father of **Methuselah**, and he had other sons and daughters. So all the days of Enoch were three hundred and sixty-five years. Enoch walked with God; and he was not, for God took him.[121]

Jared in Hebrew is *yared*, which means to come down or descend. The man characterized by "descending" becomes the father of Enoch, or Chanokh, which is "dedicated." Chanokh lived on earth 365 years before he was taken by God, which matches the number of days in a year. Chanokh fathered Methuselah (*Metushelach*), which means "a herald of arms," or more literally, "a man (male, husband) of the sword." Both components of Methuselah's name are homonyms to two other Hebrew words:

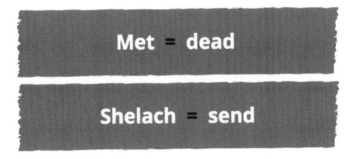

Met = dead

Shelach = send

The word shelach, which means to send out, is a common-sense root for the noun of the same spelling, which means a weapon such as a dart or sword. In Hebrew, the cognate to the English word "apostle" is *sheliach*, or "sent one." Both weapons and apostles are sent to accomplish a specific purpose or to hit a target. Hebrews 11:5 states:

121. Ge 5:18-24

By faith Enoch was translated that he
should not see death; and was not
found, because God had translated
him: for before his translation he had
this testimony, that he pleased God.
[122]

According to Munk's (p. 85) reference to *Sefer
HaYashar*, "Enoch was carried to Heaven alive, in full
view, in a fiery chariot drawn by fiery horses."

These are the men who are hidden
reefs in your love feasts when they
feast with you without fear, caring
for themselves; *clouds without water,
carried along by winds; autumn trees
without fruit, doubly dead*, uprooted;
wild waves of the sea, casting
up their own shame like foam;
wandering stars, for whom the black
darkness has been reserved forever.

It was also about these men that
Enoch, in the seventh generation
from Adam, prophesied, saying,
'Behold, the Lord came with many
thousands of His holy ones, to
execute judgment upon all, and to
convict all the ungodly of all their
ungodly deeds which they have
done in an ungodly way, and of
all the harsh things which ungodly
sinners have spoken against Him.'
These are grumblers, finding fault,
following after their own lusts;
they speak arrogantly, flattering
people for the sake of gaining an
advantage.[123]

This text in Jude is reminiscent of the genealogy of
Chanokh:

122. This
interpretation
by Jude is
supported
by rabbinic
commentaries
on Genesis
5:22 in *Vayikra
Rabbah 29*,
Onkelos,
and Targum
Yerushalmi.

123. Jude 1:12-16

6th Generation - Yared - Descending

7th Generation - Chanokh - Dedication

8th Generation - Methusaleh - Man sent with weapons

Some of the words allude to the homonyms of the genealogy: men doubly dead. By describing such men as clouds without water and autumn trees without fruit, Jude associates them with the fall feasts, both the water-pouring Sukkot ceremony, the season of rain, and the firstfruits that were offered at Sukkot. Sukkot is the seventh feast, and Chanokh was the seventh generation from Adam. In the same chapter of Leviticus, the Feast of Sukkot is described both as a seven-day feast and an eight-day feast; the eighth-day celebration is both connected to Sukkot and stands alone.

Yared means to come down, and as the sixth generation, Yared corresponds to the sixth "feast," which is actually a fast, Yom HaKippurim. It often is referred to as the holiest day of the Hebrew year, and the Lord descends to speak with the High Priest from between the two cherubim on this day. It is a day of judgment within Jewish tradition, and on this day of special intimacy with those who want to appear holy before Him, a covering is made for their souls (*nafshim*).

Although symbolically they gather in the "cloud" of rainwater in white clothes on Rosh HaShanah, the first day of the seventh month, ten days later the holy ones re-assemble for judgment so that scarlet sins may turn white. This transformation is symbolized by the white garments of Rosh HaShanah and Yom

Kippur that are worn in the synagogue. A judgment concerning the nation as well as each individual is sealed on this day when the gates close.

Four days later, still in the seventh month, this great cloud of witnesses enters Sukkot to testify to the ushpizin for seven days...or is it eight? If Sukkot symbolizes the millennial reign of Messiah, then Chanokh's name prophesies of what happens. Chanokh means dedication, but it also means the inauguration of something as well as education and training. The millennial reign is a time when the Torah will go forth from Jerusalem, educating all nations and inaugurating a period of restoration and return to the Ancient of Days to prepare for the rededication of the Creation. According to Munk (1994, p. 83), Chanokh "trained himself for holiness," and this explains his sincere walk with Elohim and eventual disappearance from the earth in the eighth generation. Sukkah 52a states: "The Evil Inclination. The schoolhouse, i.e., overcome it by your application to study."

One Jewish tradition speaks of ushpizin,[124] holy ones of old such as David, Aaron, and Joseph, who enter each sukkah during Sukkot and inquire, "How well have you dwelled in sukkot over the past year?" They are sent to inquire and to analyze each family for additional judgment. Yeshua sent (shalach) his apostles (shliachim) to minister to Israel, but if the towns did not receive them as their guests, or ushpizin, the disciples were to shake the dust of that town from their feet as a sign of judgment against them.[125]

Each patriarch represents the judgment of a spiritual quality:

- Abraham represents love and kindness
- Isaac represents restraint and personal strength
- Jacob represents beauty and truth

124. Abraham, Isaac, Jacob, Moses, Aaron, Joseph, and King David visit each sukkah. Each day of Sukkot, all seven souls are present, but each takes his turn to lead the other six Ushpizin, the Aramaic word meaning "guests."

125. Mt 10:4, Mk 6:11, Lu 9:5

- Moses represents eternality and dominance through Torah
- Aaron represents empathy and receptivity to divine splendor
- Joseph represents holiness and the spiritual foundation
- David represents the establishment of the kingdom of Heaven on Earth

Maimonides taught that collectively, the ushpizin judge the heart of the Torah:

> While eating and drinking himself, one is obligated to feed the stranger, orphan, and widow, along with the other unfortunate poor... [One who does not] is not enjoying a mitzvah,[126] but rather his stomach. (Laws of Yom Tov 6:18).

This sort of reflection and rededication is necessary before the arrival of the Eighth Day, or the Last Great Day. On the eighth day, there is no requirement to dwell in sukkot, nor are the ushpizin sent to judge the sukkah. What (or who) happens in the eighth generation?

In the genealogy, what happens is typified by Methuselah: a "husband" sent with weapons to execute the judgments. Remarkably, Jude's diatribe is against men who have celebrated the "love feasts," the *moedim* of Israel. Zechariah prophesies that all nations will be required to come up to Jerusalem for Sukkot during the millennial reign, but it is with an extension of the conditions previously placed only upon Israel: if the nations do not obey the Word, then they will not receive rain in its season. This suggests that not all who come up to celebrate and obey are truly transformed within, but doing so with hidden motives.

126.
commandment

But these men revile the things which

they do not understand; and the
things which they know *by instinct,*
like unreasoning animals, *by these
things they are destroyed.*[127]

It is an extra level of purging that is described in
Jude, for all those who assemble at the fall feasts are
not bringing first fruits, or any fruit at all, for they are
"uprooted." They are "clouds without water," who
are not to be compared with the great cloud of holy
ones returning to execute judgment. As the Torah's
letter without the Spirit is dead, so too these beasts
without the Holy Spirit that would have allowed them
to grow fruit and to rain the living water of Sukkot.

The second Sukkot of the traditional Chanukkah
celebration is not merely a celebration of dedication.
It is part of the prophecies embedded in the books
of the Torah and Prophets. When a passage of
Scripture appears to be vague about whether
Sukkot is a seven-day feast or an eight-day feast, it
is not accidental. The reader is to understand that
although judgment *yarad* (came down) and was
sealed at Yom Kippur, there is yet a process of its
execution. Those who are sealed will walk with God
like Enoch, likewise taken up for their dedication.

As it was in the days of Noah, so are the days of
Messiah's coming. Noah was the eighth generation
from Adam, and he was named Noach (rest) to
identify the Messiah's rest from violence, a "Shabbat,
Shabbat," of seventh millennium rest followed by the
eighth millennium of rest. The violent purging of the
Flood made Noah's eighth-generation rest possible.

It would involve a much lengthier study than is
possible in a booklet, but consider that the Book
of Revelation describes an additional battle and
judgment when the adversary is once again "loosed"
at the end of the millennial reign. The adversary
is permitted at the dawn of the eighth millennium
to deceive human beings, and it may be to those

"grumblers, finding fault, following after their own lusts; they speak arrogantly, flattering people for the sake of gaining an advantage" that the adversary directs his subversion. The presence of such people in the millennium will be "hidden reefs" in a world where the knowledge of the Holy One is as the waters cover the sea.[128] They are devoid of a heart for the Father's commandments or love for His Sent One, Messiah Yeshua.

128. Is 11:9; Ha 2:14

12

CONCLUSION

This booklet has been historical, investigative, analytical, and informational. The theme of Chanukkah always was intended to be inspirational. Whether to inspire the soldier terrified of death in battle or to encourage the stranger and Israelite in desperate need of a House of Prayer in which to worship, dedication and rededication in Scripture is evidence of spiritual transformation.

The soldier's sense of despair and impending doom is transformed to faith that the battle is the Holy One's, not his. His job is to walk in the faith of Abraham. The Israelite mixing holy commandments with the ways of the nations can repent and return, dedicating anew the purified personal house. The descendants of Abraham in faith are encouraged that the Great Shepherd is gathering the righteous from the nations to a House of Prayer. The priest prepares the greater House for the blessings of Sukkot even in winter, a time that Israel gathers the stranger, alien, orphan, and widow; it is not a time to scatter the friends of God.

It is Adonai's job to scatter the enemy in winter, but it is His children's job to prepare their personal temples for this great event. In this sense, the information in this booklet is more than history or analysis; it is inspiration to purify one's heart from anti-Scripture, anti-faithful thinking and doing. Chanukkah is inspiration regardless of whether a disciple of Yeshua is a native-born Israelite or among those whose first circumcision is of the heart. Chanukkah is a message of inclusion and expansion of Yeshua's Kingdom, which stirs up one's faith and increases it.

As we reflect on those things from which we have been delivered, those corpses of addiction, twisted thinking, and words of desolation that polluted the temples of our bodies, it becomes a celebration for so great a deliverance. At the Feast of Dedication, let Israel celebrate clean Temples empowered to serve the Father and His sheep.

Aren't you glad that Jews grew Chanukkah out of the Seed of the Torah?

Aren't you glad that when Yeshua conquers the Abomination that Causes Desolation that you are included...and always were included...in the battle plan?

The holy menorah represents the Seven Spirits of Adonai, and He shined on the Bread of Faces, representing all Israel in His Holy Presence. The beauty of the lighting of the menorah was that in building the Tabernacle, all Israel, both men and women, brought the holy oil. All Israel is to be crushed like the suffering servant Yeshua, dedicated to the Father's House and all who gather there to serve Him.

Israel is crushed and poured out like the olive harvest at the season of Sukkot, and at the second Sukkot, Chanukkah, there is a second celebration of thanksgiving. Jews and those who will ally themselves with the God of the Jews yield the flowing oil of dedication in gratefulness for redemption from the abominations that caused desolation.

Yeshua is the Light of the World. Yeshua commands his disciples to be the light of the world, dedicating themselves anew to His commandments in order to serve the world. Like the Maccabees of old, this generation needs to free itself from the corpses of sin and compromise that permit the enemy to overrun the Holy Temple of Messiah's Body. The sheep hear Yeshua's voice speaking the commandments of the Father. They will not listen to another.

> For this reason, they are before the throne of God; and they serve Him day and night in His temple; and He who sits on the throne will spread His tabernacle over them. They will hunger no longer, nor thirst anymore; nor will the sun beat down on them, nor any heat; *for the Lamb in the center of the throne will be their shepherd, and will guide them to springs of the water of life; and God will wipe every tear from their eyes.*
> [129]

Lord, YOU are my Light. You are my Great Shepherd. You make me a brave soldier. I dedicate my house to You, for I will live and not die. May Your Word shine through me and light the faces of all Israel...and all the world!

129. Re 7:15–17

QUESTIONS FOR REVIEW

1. What was the commission of Peter and the other apostles?

2. Which prophet prophesied about a miraculous event that would occur on the 24th of Kislev? To which of the seven feasts of Israel can the prophesied event be compared?

3. a. For what two reasons could a feast celebration have a "makeup session" or second chance to celebrate?

    b. Define a *sheni*.

4. On which Jewish celebration did Yeshua declare that his sheep would hear his voice?

5. Complete the equivalent expressions:

Lights ≈ _____

Lights ≈ _____   _____   _____

6. Compare *and* contrast Chaggai and Zechariah's prophecies.

7. Give a brief history of the "first Chanukkah."

8. a. Explain the Bible's use of consecutive numbers, such as seven and eight, to illustrate or hint to a principle in the text.

b. Explain how this use of consecutive numbers hints to the role of the seventh feast of Israel, Sukkot, and the additional celebration of Chanukkah, which is symbolized by an eight-branched menorah (nine, including the *shamash*, or "servant" candle).

9. a. Who is the Red One?

b. Explain what the Red One has to do with Jewish prayer and expectation at Chanukkah.

10. Explain how Yeshua *did* tell his doubters plainly that he was the Messiah at the Feast of Dedication and how this is Good News for the nations.

APPENDIX A

Pig on the Temple Mount

Then the king wrote to his whole kingdom that all should be one people, 42 and that all should give up their particular customs. 43 All the Gentiles accepted the command of the king. Many even from Israel gladly adopted his religion; they sacrificed to idols and profaned the sabbath. 44 And the king sent letters by messengers to Jerusalem and the towns of Judah; he directed them to follow customs strange to the land, 45 to forbid burnt offerings and sacrifices and drink offerings in the sanctuary, to profane sabbaths and festivals, 46 to defile the sanctuary and the priests, 47 to build altars and sacred precincts and shrines for idols, to sacrifice swine and other unclean animals, 48 and to leave their sons uncircumcised. They were to make themselves abominable by everything unclean and profane, 49 so that they would forget the law and change all the ordinances. 50 He added, "And whoever does not obey the command of the king shall die." (1 Mac 1:41–50)

APPENDIX B

Supernatural Fire

In the books of the Maccabees that document the history of the war against Hellenist Jews and Greeks, another account documents a supernatural fire that lit the rededicated altar when the Jews returned from captivity in Babylon. This dedication fire was fueled by the residue of the hidden fire from the original altar:

> For when our ancestors were being led captive to Persia, the pious priests of that time took some of the fire of the altar and secretly hid it in the hollow of a dry cistern, where they took such precautions that the place was unknown to anyone. But after many years had passed, when it pleased God, Nehemiah, having been commissioned by the king of Persia, sent the descendants of the priests who had hidden the fire to get it. And when they reported to us that they had not found fire but only a thick liquid, he ordered them to dip it out and bring it. When the materials for the sacrifices were presented, Nehemiah ordered the priests to sprinkle the liquid on the wood and on the things laid upon it. When this had been done and some time had passed, and when the sun, which had been clouded over, shone out, a great fire blazed up, so that all marveled. (2 Mac 1:19-22)

The symbolism of the combustion fueled by the fire from the former altar is significant. Those who returned wept because they remembered the glory of the former Temple. Although conquered and deported, they had miraculously returned to the House and repented. Although cast away, the same "lights" of a remnant few of the righteous priests returned to consecrate the altar.

In closing the invitation to Jews to celebrate Chanukkah, the writer connects the celebration with miraculous fire of the first Temple dedication of eight days:

> Then the Lord will disclose these things, and the glory of the Lord and the cloud will appear, as they were shown in the case of Moses, and as Solomon asked that the place should be specially consecrated. It was also made clear that being possessed of wisdom Solomon offered sacrifice for the dedication and completion of the temple. Just as Moses prayed to the Lord, and fire came down from heaven and consumed the sacrifices, so also Solomon prayed, and the fire came down and consumed the whole burnt offerings. And Moses said, "They were consumed because the sin offering had not been eaten." Likewise Solomon also kept the eight days. (2 Mac 2:8-12)

The context is a description of the apocalyptic return of the cloud in the last day when the hidden ark will be revealed. The text continues with apocalyptic appeal:

> Since, therefore, we are about to celebrate the purification, we write to you. Will you therefore please keep the days? It is God who has saved all his people, and has returned the inheritance to all, and the kingship and the priesthood and the consecration, as he promised through the law. We have hope in God that he will soon have mercy on us and *will gather us from everywhere under heaven into his holy place*, for he has rescued us from great evils and has purified the place. (2 Mac 2:16-18)

The writer's focus on the return of the kingship, priesthood, and consecration through the Torah is paired with an expectation of return from everywhere under heaven. When the Pharisees challenged Yeshua to tell plainly if he were the Messiah at Chanukkah, they would have known these expectations recorded by the scribes.

While they wanted a Chanukkah Messianic kingship and a righteous priesthood restored according to Torah law, Yeshua instead focused on the gathering from everywhere under Heaven, a detail seen only in minimal fulfillment with the 1st Century Jewish proselytes. Those who gathered at the House in Acts Two were a small representation of the worldwide gathering promised by the Prophets of Israel.

APPENDIX C

Chanukkah as a Sukkot Sheni

10 Now Maccabeus and his followers, the Lord leading them
on, recovered the temple and the city; 2 they tore down the
altars that had been built in the public square by the foreigners,
and also destroyed the sacred precincts. 3 They purified the
sanctuary, and made another altar of sacrifice; then, striking fire
out of flint, they offered sacrifices, after a lapse of two years, and
they offered incense and lighted lamps and set out the bread
of the Presence. 4 When they had done this, they fell prostrate
and implored the Lord that they might never again fall into
such misfortunes, but that, if they should ever sin, they might be
disciplined by him with forbearance and not be handed over to
blasphemous and barbarous nations. 5 It happened that on the
same day on which the sanctuary had been profaned by the
foreigners, the purification of the sanctuary took place, that is,
on the twenty-fifth day of the same month, which was Chislev.
6 They celebrated it for eight days with rejoicing, in the manner
of the festival of booths, remembering how not long before,
during the festival of booths, they had been wandering in the
mountains and caves like wild animals. 7 Therefore, carrying
ivy-wreathed wands and beautiful branches and also fronds of
palm, they offered hymns of thanksgiving to him who had given
success to the purifying of his own holy place. 8 They decreed
by public edict, ratified by vote, that the whole nation of the
Jews should observe these days every year. 9 Such then was
the end of Antiochus, who was called Epiphanes. (2 Mac 10:1–9
NRSV)

APPENDIX D

Talmudic Thoughts on the Evil Inclination, Seven Shepherds, and Eight Princes from Mas. Sukkah 52a

- And the land shall mourn, every family apart; the family of the house of David apart, and their wives apart. Is it not, they said, an *a fortiori* argument? If in the future when they will be engaged in mourning and the Evil Inclination will have no power over them, the Torah nevertheless says, men separately and women separately, how much more so now when they are engaged in rejoicing and the Evil Inclination has sway over them. What is the cause of the mourning [mentioned in the last cited verse]?...One explained, the cause is the slaying of Messiah the son of Joseph, another explained, the cause is the slaying of the Evil Inclination.

- It is well according to him who explains that the cause is the slaying of Messiah the son of Joseph, since that well agrees with the Scriptural verse, "And they shall look upon me because they have thrust him through, and they shall mourn for him as one mourns for his only son"; but according to him who explains the cause to be the slaying of the Evil Inclination, is this [it may be objected] an occasion for mourning? Is it not rather an occasion for rejoicing? Why then should they weep? R. Judah expounded: In the time to come the Holy One, blessed be He, will bring the Evil Inclination and slay it in the presence of the righteous and the wicked. To the righteous it will have the appearance of a towering hill, and to the wicked it will have the appearance of a hair thread. Both the former and the latter will weep; the righteous will weep saying, 'How were we able to overcome such a towering hill!' The wicked also will weep saying, 'How is it that we were unable to conquer this hair thread!'

- R. Assi stated, The Evil Inclination is at first like the thread of a spider, but ultimately— R. Dosa and the Rabbis and they becomes like cart ropes, as it is said, Woe unto them that draw iniquity with cords of vanity, and sin as it were with a cart-rope. Our Rabbis taught, The Holy One, blessed be He, will say to the Messiah, the son of David (May he reveal himself speedily in our days!), 'Ask of me anything, and I will give it to thee', as it is said, I will tell of the decree etc. this day have I begotten thee, ask of me and I will give the nations for thy inheritance.

- But when he will see that the Messiah the son of Joseph is slain, he will say to Him, 'Lord of the Universe, I ask of Thee only the gift of life'. 'As to life', He would answer him, 'Your father David has already prophesied this concerning you', as it is said, He asked life of thee, thou gavest it him, [even length of days for ever and ever].

- R. 'Awira or, as some say, R. Joshua b. Levi, made the following exposition: **The Evil Inclination has seven names**.

- The Holy One, blessed be He, called it **Evil**, as it is said, For the imagination of man's heart is evil from his youth...therefore the foreskin of your heart.

- Only Moses called it [the Evil Inclination] **the Uncircumcised**

- David called it **Unclean**, as it is said, Create me a clean heart, which implies that there is an unclean one.

- Solomon called it **the Enemy**...

- Isaiah called it **the Stumbling-Block**, as it is

- Ezekiel called it **Stone**, as it is said, "And I will take away the heart of stone...."

- Joel called it **the Hidden One**

- And this shall be peace: when the Assyrian shall come into our land, and when he shall tread in our palaces, then shall we raise up against him **seven shepherds and eight princes** among men. Who are the 'seven shepherds'? — David in the middle, Adam, Seth and Methuselah and Abraham, Jacob and Moses. And who are the eight princes? Jesse, Saul, Samuel, Amos, Zephaniah, Zedekiah, **the Messiah**[130], and Elijah.

130. Texts disagree on whether Elijah precedes Messiah or Messiah precedes Elijah as 7-8.

APPENDIX E

Mo. #	Post-Babylonian Calendar	Meaning of Months	Theme of Month (Babylonian & Biblical)
1	Nisan	Their flight	Redemption Miracles
2	Iyyar	(natural) healing	Introspection, Self improvement
3	Sivan	Bright - their covering	Giving of Torah
4	Tammuz	Hidden - giver of the vine (also a Phoenician deity)	Sin of the Golden Calf, guarding of the eyes
5	Av	Father	Av the Comforter
6	Elul	A vain thing - nothingness	Repentance
7	Tishrei	Beginning (from reishit)	Month of the Strong or Month of the Ancients
8	Cheshvan	Eighth	The Flood
9	Kislev	Security, trust	(Restful) Sleep
10	Tevet	Good (from tov)	Divine Grace
11	Shevat	unknown	Tree of Life
12	Adar	Strength	Good Success

Correlation of Months[131]

Biblical Calendar	Meaning of Biblical Months (Harvesting Schedule)	Biblical Feasts
Abib	**Ripening of grains** Barley, Wheat	Passover, Unleavened Bread, Firstfruits
Ziv	**Splendor** or **Radiance** [Flowers] (Barley harvest)	
3rd	(Wheat harvest)	Feast of Weeks
4th		
5th		
6th	(Fruit harvest)	
Ethanim	**Ever-flowing streams**	Rosh HaShanah (Trumpets), Yom Kippur, Sukkot
Bul	**Produce** (in the sense of rain)	
9th		
10th		
11th		
12th		

131. Based on ben Avraham's model. See References (2003) to locate original chart.

REFERENCES

Adler, R. *Are We Witnessing the Restoration of an Ancient Biblical Status for Non-Jews?* January 15, 2017. Breaking Israel News. Retrieved from: https://www.breakingisraelnews. com/82061/seeing-restoration-ancient-biblical-status-non-jews/#2YkLmBfpbK4iLW8E.99

Ben Avraham, D. (2012). *Bnei Avraham Ahuvecha: gerim in Chassidic thought.* Charleston: Createspace.

Ben Avraham, Y. (2003, March 3). Hebrew day and month names. Posted to YashaNet. Retrieved 10/22/2016 from http://www.yashanet.com/library/hebrew-days-and-months.html

Eisenberg, R. (2010). *Jewish traditions: a JPS guide.* New York: Jewish Publication Society.

Fohrman, D. (2016). "Reindeer and Latkes: Aren't the Holidays Suspiciously Similar?" Audio lecture. Aleph Beta Academy. https://www.alephbeta.org/course/lecture/chanukah-5777-2016/autoplay

The Holy Bible: New Revised Standard Version. 1989. Nashville: Thomas Nelson Publishers.

Mitchell, D. (2016). *Messiah ben Joseph.* Newton Mearns, Scotland: Campbell Publications.

Munk, E. 2001. (E.S. Mazer, Trans.) *The call of the Torah: an anthology of interpretation and commentary on the Five Books of Moses.* Vol. Bereishis. New York: Mesorah Publications, Ltd.

Ryken, L., Wilhoit, J., & Longman, (Eds.). (1998). *Dictionary of Biblical imagery.* Downer's Grove, IL: InterVarsity Press.

Scherman, N., (Ed.). (1996). *The Complete Artscroll Siddur.* Nusach Sefard - Pocket Size Edition. New York: Mesorah Publications, Ltd.

Schwarz, H. (2006). *Tree of Souls: The Mythology of Judaism*. "The Seven Shepherds." Oxford University Press.

The Targums of Onkelos and Jonathan Ben Uzziel on the Pentateuch with the fragments of the Jerusalem Targum from the Chaldee. J. W. Etheridge, Trans. 1862. http://targum.info/pj/pjgen18-22.htm. Retrieved 1/15/17.

Thomas, R. L. (1998). *New American Standard Hebrew-Aramaic and Greek dictionaries : Updated edition*. Anaheim: Foundation Publications, Inc.

ABOUT THE AUTHOR

Dr. Hollisa Alewine has her B.S. and M.Ed. from Texas A&M and a Doctorate from Oxford Graduate School; she is the author of Standing with Israel: A House of Prayer for All Nations, The Creation Gospel Bible study series, and a programmer on Hebraic Roots Network. Dr. Alewine is a student and teacher of the Word of God.

68207727R00076

Made in the USA
Lexington, KY
04 October 2017